The Common Pursuit

SIMON GRAY

The Common Pursuit

Scenes from the Literary Life

☐ ☐ ☐ ☐

Methuen · London and New York

For Ben and Lucy

THE COMMON PURSUIT was first presented by the Lyric Theatre at the Lyric Theatre, London, on June 28, 1984, with the following cast:

STUART	Nicholas Le Provost
MARIGOLD	Nina Thomas
MARTIN	Ian Ogilvy
HUMPHRY	Clive Francis
NICK	Robert East
PETER	Simon Williams

Directed by Harold Pinter
Designed by Eileen Diss
Lighting by Dave Horn

The American premiere of the play took place at the Long Wharf Theatre (Artistic Director, Arvin Brown; Executive Director, M. Edgar Rosenblum), New Haven, on January 11, 1985, with the following cast:

STUART	William Converse Roberts
MARIGOLD	Ellen Parker
MARTIN	Michael Countryman
HUMPHRY	Peter Friedman
NICK	Nathan Lane
PETER	Mark Arnott

Directed by Kenneth Frankel
Set Design by David Jenkins
Costumes by David Murin
Lighting by Pat Collins
Production Stage Manager: Ann Keefe

Presented by John A. McQuiggan in association with the Hart Entertainment Group and Douglas M. Lawson, the New York premiere of the play took place at the Promenade Theatre on October 19, 1986 with the following cast:

STUART THORNE	Kristoffer Tabori
MARIGOLD WATSON	Judy Geeson
MARTIN MUSGROVE	Michael Countryman
HUMPHRY TAYLOR	Peter Friedman
NICK FINCHLING	Nathan Lane
PETER WHETWORTH	Dylan Baker

Directed by Simon Gray and Michael McGuire
Settings by David Jenkins
Costumes by David Murin
Lighting by Frances Aronson
Production Stage Manager: Lois Griffing

The Common Pursuit

CHARACTERS

STUART

MARIGOLD

MARTIN

HUMPHRY

NICK

PETER

ACT ONE

ACT 1

SCENE 1

STUART's *room in Cambridge. Twenty years ago. The gramaphone is playing.* STUART *is seated at his desk, a letter in his hands.* MARIGOLD *is lying on the bed reading a book*

STUART *(Referring to letter):* I just don't know.

MARIGOLD *(Looking up at him):* What is it?

STUART: A letter from Dr. Leavis. I wrote telling him I was thinking of calling the magazine *The Common Pursuit.* In homage to his book. He says I can publish it in my first issue, if I want.

MARIGOLD: That's terrific, isn't it.

STUART: Yes, but he says I have to publish the whole letter, and the trouble is it's full of qualifications, rather long and depressing qualifications actually, about my chances of making a success of it—full of words like "embattled" and "beleaguered"—it makes the magazine seem on the point of surrender before it's even begun. But on the other hand, to have his name in the very first issue would certainly attract a lot of attention, wouldn't it?

MARIGOLD: Yes, I'm sure it would.

(MARIGOLD *smiles at* STUART. STUART *smiles back. Picks up a typescript, then looks toward* MARIGOLD *again. She has*

3

turned away. He continues to look at her, then opens a drawer, takes a letter out, looks it over)

MARIGOLD: Hey what's that?

STUART: I rather think, from the way that it goes into all sorts of details about my private person, that it must be a letter from you. Yes, it is from you. You're the only person in the world who knows enough about me to have written this postscript. I couldn't possibly read it out to you—your whole body would turn pink with embarrassment. And here's your name, Marigold Watson. That is your name, isn't it?

MARIGOLD: You're meant to be reading poems and articles and such stuff. Not sex-crazed communications from the likes of me.

STUART *(Crosses to her and sits next to her on the bed):* I just wanted to make absolutely sure that I'm trapped in my room with the most disgusting girl in Cambridge. You are Marigold Watson, aren't you? The most disgusting girl in Cambridge.

(They kiss)

MARIGOLD: Oh Stuart, Stuart, Stuart. If you are Stuart Thorne, that is. The most disgusting man in Cambridge.

(They kiss again. He starts to unbutton her shirt. MARTIN appears at the doorway, stops, watches a moment, then withdraws hurriedly)

STUART: Oh Christ, we can't.

MARIGOLD: Why not?

STUART: I've got some people coming.

MARIGOLD: What people?

STUART: All the types I've invited to help me with the magazine. Nick, and Captain Marvel, and the chap who sent me those terrific poems, Humphry Taylor, and some peculiar freak who actually wants to work on the financial side. I can't remember his name—I've invited them all for coffee *(Looks at his watch)* in ten minutes.

MARIGOLD: That's all right. We'll be extremely quick. Like lightning. We'll be finished long before they arrive.

STUART: But I don't want to be extremely quick. Like lightning. I want to be extremely slow. *(Pause)* Forever, in fact.

MARIGOLD *(After a small pause):* Forever?

STUART: Forever. But that doesn't mean I can't be extremely quick too.

(They start to make love)

MARIGOLD: Oh, the door.

STUART: Oh, yes. *(He crosses to door, closes it, then crosses to curtains, makes to draw them, looks out of window, stops)* Christ! It's—it's Stout! *(Pointing)*

5

MARIGOLD: Stout?

STUART: Hubert Stout! The poet. And that must be his wife . . . Charlotte. They've only just married. But where are they going? Oh, into one of the guest rooms. They must be staying the night. We've got to talk to him! Tell him about the magazine. Actually to see Hubert Stout. Today of all days. It's like an omen. A portent!

MARIGOLD: But I thought that you were going to ravish my body?

STUART: Yes, well I will. Ravish and ravish and ravish. Later. But now—

MARIGOLD: Do you want me to come like this, or would he prefer me with clothes on?

STUART: Probably like that given his reputation.

(STUART *crosses to his desk to get his jacket.* MARIGOLD *starts to dress. He checks papers on his desk, speaking to himself*)

STUART: I'll show him Grimsby's short stories, Humphry Taylor's poems—Where are they?—and the first draft of the editorial. I better show him Leavis' letter, too.

(STUART *turns to* MARIGOLD *as she finishes dressing; then both cross to door. He opens door and runs into* MARTIN *in hallway, backs into room speaking to* MARTIN)

STUART: Oh—hello. Um . . . um . . . come in.

6

Act One

(MARTIN *enters*)

STUART: This is um, um this is—

MARTIN: Martin Musgrove.

MARIGOLD *(Embarrassed):* Hello.

MARTIN: Isn't there going to be a meeting about the magazine then?

STUART: Yes, but look, I'm terribly sorry, we won't be a minute, actually, but there's somebody we've got to see urgently—make yourself at home. And tell anyone else who shows up we'll be right back.

MARTIN: Oh right.

STUART *(Gestures):* Put a record on, if you want.

(STUART *goes off with* MARIGOLD. MARTIN *stands uncertainly. He leans the folder he is carrying against the bureau and looks at the gramaphone, on top of which is a record sleeve. He reads the title of the work, nods, puts the record on. Holding on to the cover, he wanders over to the desk, glances at the typescripts, etc., sees a letter, picks it up, and furtively begins to read it. He goes to the window to read it by the light, glances out the window, dashes in a panic to the desk, puts the letter on it, dashes to the bureau, picks up folder, starts to sit on bed, rushes back to window, sits down, assumes a listening posture.* HUMPHRY *appears at the door.* MARTIN *is too absorbed to be aware of him)*

HUMPHRY *(Entering properly):* Stuart Thorne not here then?

MARTIN *(Starting):* Oh. No, they've just dashed off somewhere. But they'll be back in a moment. He said to wait.

(HUMPHRY *sits down. There is a pause)*

MARTIN: Marvelous stuff, isn't it?

(HUMPHRY *grunts)*

MARTIN: Do you like Vivaldi?

HUMPHRY: Yes. But I like Bach more. Which this is.

MARTIN: Really? Are you sure?

HUMPHRY: Yes.

MARTIN: Oh. Well, you're probably right. I had some idea it was that Vivaldi piece in F major—which Bach is it then, do you know?

HUMPHRY: No.

MARTIN: It sounds terribly like Vivaldi to me.

(HUMPHRY *gets up, goes over to it. He deftly stops the gramaphone, removes the record, and looks around for the sleeve)*

MARTIN: What is it precisely?

HUMPHRY *(Glances at the record):* The Suite Number Three.

MARTIN: Vivaldi, you mean?

HUMPHRY *(Picks up the correct sleeve from the bureau and slips the record in):* No, Bach of course.

MARTIN: Really! You must have a terrific feeling for music. I only recognize stuff when I've heard it hundreds of times before. And then I get it wrong, it turns out. *(He laughs)* You're Humphry Wentworth, aren't you?

HUMPHRY: Taylor. Humphry Taylor.

MARTIN: Taylor, yes. And you're doing history, aren't you?

HUMPHRY: Moral sciences.

MARTIN: Oh, of course. But in your *last* year, aren't you?

HUMPHRY: Second year.

MARTIN: Ah. Well, I'm Martin Musgrove. I'm second-year too. In English. Stuart told me you were interested in his new literary magazine. I think it's a terrific idea, don't you? Just what Cambridge needs, a new literary magazine. He said he was thinking of calling it *The Common Pursuit* after that book—you know—called—uh—

HUMPHRY: The Common Pursuit.

MARTIN: That's the one, yes. *(Little laugh)* Are you going to help him edit it?

HUMPHRY: I doubt it. One editor is usually more than enough.

(Pause)

MARTIN: Oh, I see what you mean. Quarrels and things like that. Have you written something for it?

HUMPHRY: I sent in some poems. What about you? Have you written anything?

MARTIN: Oh, no—well, I did submit a little thing. A sort of prose poem about well, cats, actually. *(He laughs)* But Stuart sent it back saying I had far more grasp of cats than I did of poetry—or prose—so I'd better stick to those. Quite right, of course. It was pretty embarrassing when I read it through. I haven't got any talent at all, you see. But I'm interested in publishing, so I want to work on the magazine from that point of view. The business side, you know, helping with subscriptions, advertising, raising money, anything of that sort. Is he going to publish your poems?

HUMPHRY: No. I've come to get them back.

MARTIN: Oh. What didn't he like about them?

HUMPHRY: He liked them. It's me. I don't like them.

MARTIN: Really, why not?

HUMPHRY: Because they make me feel sick. In fact, I've decided to give up writing. Poetry, anyway.

MARTIN: But mightn't you eventually write some that don't make you feel sick?

HUMPHRY: Possibly. But it's not worth the risk. Besides, I'm going to be a professional philosopher. So I'll have to concentrate on thinking until I've got my first-class degree and a job in a university.

MARTIN: That's what you want, is it?

HUMPHRY: I haven't any choice. As you can't be a professional philosopher except in a university.

MARTIN: Do you want to be in any particular university?

HUMPHRY: This one will do.

MARTIN *(Laughs slightly):* Any particular college?

HUMPHRY: This one will do.

MARTIN: Well—that's quite a prediction, really.

HUMPHRY: It wasn't meant to be. More like an obituary in fact. But if I'm going to institutionalize myself, I suppose I might as well do it in one of the better institutions.

MARTIN: I wish I had that sort of confidence about my own future. I only thought of publishing because I can't think of anything else.

11

(NICK *enters, coughing slightly. Looks around*)

NICK: Where's Stuart?

MARTIN: He'll be back in a minute. He said we were to wait.

NICK: Well, isn't there any coffee on the go or anything? I've got a hangover.

MARTIN: Really? How did you get it?

NICK: I think it might have been because I drank too much. In fact, look, what's that stuff—slimy, thick, and yellow?

HUMPHRY: That covers a large number of revolting substances.

MARTIN: Oh, it must be avocat, mustn't it? A sort of eggnog.

NICK: That explains it. I'm allergic to eggs. Probably allergic to nogs too. If they're what they sound like. It was that bloody girl from Girton—Harriet whatsit?

MARTIN: Hofstadt?

NICK: Yes, she produced it. I was perfectly all right until then. Coasting along on white wine, martini, rum, Scotch, that sort of thing. But then that's Harriet, always there when you least want her, passing out eggnogs when you least want them; she should have been a nurse.

12

(NICK *laughs and coughs slightly*)

MARTIN: Did Harriet give the party?

NICK: Do you think I'd go to a party given by Harriet Hofstadt? No, no, it was some prick, prickette from King's, secretary of their literary society, Jeremy—

MARTIN: Jeremy Prince.

NICK: To meet that woman who's written a novel about her menstrual cycle, *Murdering.*

MARTIN: *Mothering,* isn't it?

NICK: What?

MARTIN: Isn't it *Mothering,* not *Murdering?*

NICK: I thought they were synonyms.

MARTIN *(Laughs):* Angela Thark.

NICK: What?

MARTIN: That's her name. The novelist's, isn't it? Angela Thark. I wish I'd met her. I got the novel just yesterday; I haven't read it yet. What's she like?

NICK: Much sexier than her prose. Bit of a knockout really. If you like long legs, big breasts, that sort of thing. I do. But I'm not very selective yet. I'm still a virgin. What

13

about you two? Actually, this room reeks of passion. What were you two up to before I came in?

(NICK *laughs, coughs slightly and meets* HUMPHRY's *eyes)*

MARTIN: Did she have anything interesting to say?

NICK: Who?

MARTIN: Angela Thark. Did she talk about novel writing, that sort of thing?

NICK: Look, could you hold on the incisive questions, just for a moment? I'm about to do something exceptionally difficult. *(He takes out a cigarette, lights it, and inhales)* Oh, yes, here they come, the little buggers, bobbing from iris to pupil and back again. Now the ripples of giddiness —turning into tidal bloody waves of nausea. *(He groans. Coughs)*

MARTIN: Is it always like this when you smoke a cigarette?

NICK: Only the first.

HUMPHRY: Why have it then?

NICK: So I can get on to my next. By the third or fourth I won't even notice I'm smoking.

MARTIN: But if the first few are so ghastly, and you don't even notice the rest of them, why don't you just give up?

NICK: What for?

14

HUMPHRY: For one thing, you might live longer.

NICK: Oh, you don't live longer, it just seems longer. As Sam Goldwyn said. *(To* HUMPHRY*)* One of the poets anyway. *(He wanders to the table, picks up the typescripts, etc.)*

MARTIN: You know, sometimes I think I'm missing out on addiction. I've never been addicted to anything in my life. Not even when I was a child. I mean, I'm normal all the time, which is very boring. For everyone else as well as me. While for you I suppose normal's something you accelerate away from with drinks and cigarettes . . .

NICK *(Reads out):* "Boys on their river banks, naked in the sad and dewey dawn." *(Laughs, coughs slightly)* God, I hate queer literature. *(Reads again)* The enclosed poems are not for publication, at least at this stage, but glad to hear of new magazine, hope it will be noted not only for its critical rigor, vigor, rigor, but also for its delicate insensitive poetry—delicate insensitive—*(Looks closer)*—oh, delicate *and* sensitive—pity, who's it from? Ah, James Harrop, New College, *Oxford!* Oh, that explains it, probably not even queer, just Oxford, I knew a Harrop at prep school, Nappies we used to call him. Nappies Harrop. He had to wear them at night because he was an inveterate bed-wetter. Wonder if it's the same one; he was a creep, too. *(Picks up another letter)* Ahhh . . . *(This is the letter* MARTIN *read earlier)*

HUMPHRY: You shouldn't do that.

15

NICK *(Whistles):* I say. She can really turn it on, old Mari-gold. A little overwritten, if you ask me, but I suppose that's the problem with having an affair with a literary editor. Keeping her prose up to snuff.

HUMPHRY: I said don't do that.

MARTIN: Yes, well—I must say I've never seen anyone read anyone's private letters before, you know.

NICK: Of course, you haven't. This is a notable break-through. Doing it in public, so to speak. *(Turns the last page)*

HUMPHRY: That's two warnings. You don't get a third.

NICK: Actually it's from the Dean inviting him to pay last term's wine bill.

MARTIN: No, it's not.

NICK: How do you know?

(NICK *and* HUMPHRY *look at* MARTIN)

MARTIN: Well, it's handwritten! And pages long.

NICK: Well, you know the Dean. Anything to make a con-quest. Or settle an account.

HUMPHRY *(Stands):* Are you going to put it down?

NICK: Are you going to make me?

16

HUMPHRY: If I have to. *(Crosses toward* NICK. NICK *quickly tosses the letter on the desk)*

NICK: It's time I introduced myself. I'm Nick Finchling, special agent. I've adopted this flamboyant personality as a disguise. I'm trying to find ways of persuading Stuart to publish my *Poems of Passion,* written in my late adolescence. But he says I'm still too close to them to be able to revise them properly. So, I'll do the theater criticism, as I intend to be the *Sunday Times* theater critic when I grow up. Would you really have hit me a moment ago?

HUMPHRY: The moment hasn't passed.

NICK: You're Humphry Taylor, aren't you, the philosopher poet. I've decided we're going to be friends. It's safer. *(He laughs)* Actually, Stuart says your poems have genius. And that you're a real find. *(To* MARTIN) Who are you—oh, I know, the millionaire orphan, aren't you?

MARTIN: Well, I'm not a millionaire.

NICK: But everybody says you're quite rich and if you're an orphan, you'll need a friend. *(He embraces* MARTIN) I'm your man. I'm the opposite of an orphan. I've got six parents in all, if you include the steps and ex-steps.

(PETER *enters)*

NICK: Shazam! Captain Marvel.

PETER: Sorry I'm late. I had a supervision. Where's Stuart then?

17

NICK: We're patiently waiting for him. Meanwhile—meet the poet, philosopher, and pugilist, Humphry Taylor, and that chap who wrote the charming little piece about cats that Stuart showed us. Before rejecting it.

MARTIN: Martin. Martin Musgrove.

NICK: And this is Peter Whetworth. Known as Captain Marvel from the American comic book because of the way he handles the ladies. Senior scholar in history, future Fellow of the college, and consequently one of my closest friends. Why didn't you come Angela Tharking last night?

PETER *(Who has smiled and nodded at* HUMPHRY *and* MARTIN): Oh yes. Sorry. I met up with some people.

NICK: Female people, I suppose. More than one female people?

PETER: There were two to begin with, but I whittled them down to one. Actually, I got the wrong one, as the one I whittled turned out to be the one I wanted—given the one I ended up with.

NICK: Not Ghastly Erika?

PETER: Ghastly Erika?

NICK: Well, I think her name is Erika, and she's certainly ghastly. You met her in my room last week, when I was rounding up some hopefuls, to sacrifice my virginity to.

18

PETER: Oh yes, I remember. Very, very pretty.

NICK: Exactly. In fact, your usual type. Would you like to meet her again?

PETER: I wouldn't mind.

NICK: Right. I'll arrange it.

PETER: Thanks.

MARTIN: Are you going to write for *The Common Pursuit?*

PETER: I don't know if Stuart would be interested in the kind of stuff I write.

HUMPHRY: I heard your paper. The one you gave to the college History Society.

PETER: Really? What did you think?

HUMPHRY: It had one or two good things in it. Even some originality. Especially in the first few pages.

PETER: Oh, you objected to the stuff on Professor Woodruff at the end, then, did you? I was afraid some people would. Perhaps I went a bit too far—

HUMPHRY: You didn't go nearly far enough.

PETER: Yes, I know, but there's a slight problem you see. Old Woodruff's been very nice to me—in fact, he got me my scholarship—and I do really admire his work, in a way.

HUMPHRY: Yes, well that's the wrong way, isn't it? If you admired him in the right way, you'd have paid him the compliment of arguing with him properly, wouldn't you? Besides, you introduced Schopenhauer when it was too late to count, made one or two striking points about him, and then just closed the whole argument down.

PETER: Yes, wasn't that terrible. Thank God, nobody else seemed to notice. The trouble is I kept getting interrupted before I'd finished, by this person and that—you know how it is—so I had to scribble out the last few paragraphs an hour before I actually gave the paper—a pity really. I'd like to have thought it through more thoroughly.

HUMPHRY: If you want to discuss it further, my rooms are just around the corner; Neville's Court, C staircase . . .

NICK *(Interrupting):* Have you two finished? Because I want to hear about last night. *(To* PETER*)* What you did with that girl. I'm anxious to acquire any information I can on this sex business. All I'm sure of at the moment is that I'm not queer. So what did you do with her? Did you take her back? Or get her to take you to her place? Or what? How? When? Where? With illustrations. If you don't tell me, I won't invite Ghastly Erika back for you, after all. So, come on then! What did you do with her?

PETER: Oh, nothing special.

NICK: But you took her to bed?

PETER: Of course. What else could I do with her?

NICK: Well, how did you manage it?

PETER: Manage what?

NICK: How did you persuade her? That's what I need to know. I mean, what sort of thing does one say?

PETER: Well, I gave her a cup of tea and a biscuit, and said, "Let's go to bed."

NICK: A cup of tea and a biscuit! What did you put in the tea? Or was it in the biscuit?

HUMPHRY: Excuse me, can we have some music? If we're going to wait, could we at least do something worthwhile?

NICK: I advise you not to resist him. He has a powerful personality. He nearly knocked me down just before you came in. What would you like to hear, sir?

HUMPHRY: Wagner would probably be the most inappropriate. So let's have him.

NICK: I don't know if Stuart goes in for Wagner, sir. Or anything musical really, sir. Except for seducing Marigold with, sir. Ah—I've found some.

(Takes record from MARTIN, *puts it on the gramaphone, lights a cigarette, coughs, sits on bed. They settle back and start to listen)*

21

PETER *(To* NICK): So tell me some more about Ghastly Erika . . .

NICK *(Makes to speak, is frozen by a look from* HUMPHRY, *looks at* PETER): Sssssh! *(Putting a finger to his lips.)*

Wagner fills the room. NICK *lays back on bed.* HUMPHRY *listens.* MARTIN *assumes his listening posture.* PETER *listens idly, smiling pleasantly. They remain in that position as the set goes off, the music still playing while* STUART'S *office moves on)*

SCENE 2

Late Spring. Early summer. STUART'S *office in Holborn. Nine years later. Late morning. The office is large and could be handsome. But it is dingy. There is a desk with a telephone on it. An armchair, a sofa, a cupboard. A few glasses and half-filled bottles of wine are on the shelves, as if left over from a party.*

STUART *is sitting at his desk, reading a typescript. He thinks, checks the front of the manuscript he's been reading for a number, finds it, dials the phone.*

STUART: May I speak to Mr. Stout, please. Oh, Charlotte, hello. It's Stuart Thorne, here. I was just wondering if I might have a word with Hubert. Oh is he, I'm sorry to hear that. No, I won't keep him long, I promise. *(Pause)* Hubert, it's Stuart. Charlotte says you're still a bit under the weather, and I mustn't keep you long, so I'll come straight to the point. I've just been rereading the poems you sent me, and I was wondering whether you'd come to a decision about letting me publish them. *(Stops)* What! Where did you hear that? *(Pause)* No, that's just *gossip,* Hubert, there's not the slightest chance *The Common Pursuit* is going to fold—in fact, at this very minute the Arts Council is making a formal decision to award us a substantial grant at last. It'll more than cover the debts— *(Little pause) Absolutely* sure. Peter Whetworth is on the committee. You must have met him—he's an old friend of mine from Cambridge days. He teaches history at Oxford now. The one everybody calls Captain Marvel. Yes. With the very pretty wife. Erika, yes. Anyway, he's on the committee, and he's virtually my representative. So, you see our survival is guaranteed. Of course, I'm delighted you're so pleased—but what do you say about my doing the poems. Thank you, Hubert. You won't regret it, I promise you. Well, I'll get them into proof this week, and I'll bring them over to you myself—we can correct them together if you like.

(MARTIN *enters*)

STUART: What—oh right. Well, thanks again, Hubert. Really thanks. And love to Charlotte. *(Hangs up)* I've got them.

MARTIN: What?

STUART: Hubert Stout's new poems. All six of them.

23

MARTIN: Well, that's terrific. You know, I had a feeling we'd have something to celebrate.

STUART: Eight years and thirty-one issues. And most of them have been pretty good, I think. Not all of them, of course. Not even any of them completely from cover to cover. There's always something I've let by that I didn't quite believe in. The first poems of Dougan and O'Leary, for instance, were an unforgivable mistake. Oh, do you know they sent some more of their stuff just the other day? It arrived in a weird brown parcel that looked as if it were throbbing. I thought at first it might be a letter bomb. From a rejected contributor. Or a gang of Marxist critics. But it was worse than a letter bomb. It was the latest poems of Dougan and O'Leary. And what was worse was that they were worse than the last bunch I sent back, which were worse than the ones I should have never published in the first place. But the point is—Dougan and O'Leary aside, along with say a few doubtful short stories here and one or two inadequate or overwritten articles there—I've put out thirty-one pretty good issues, actually discovered three, no, two good new writers, one very decent one, but I've never produced an issue that in my heart of hearts I consider to be a great one. The next one will be. And right at the center will be Hubert's six poems. A great issue. That's my point.

(Phone rings)

STUART: Captain Marvel! Or more likely the printers, the stationers, or old Giorgio.

MARTIN: Giorgio?

STUART: The landlord. I can't pay any of them. *(Answers the phone in Irish accent)* Good morning to you. *(To MARTIN)* Giorgio. *(To phone)* That's right, the offices of *The Common Pursuit*, yes. *(Pause)* Stuart Thorne? No, I'm afraid he's not here, nobody else either. Oh, my name's Dougan, that's right, Dougan O'Leary, sir. A poet from Belfast passing through London on his way to Dublin, and a great admirer of *The Common Pursuit,* sir, famed across the waters for its high critical standards and its undeniable integrity, so I dropped in on the off-chance to give my salutes, sir . . . Oh, I'll be glad to, yes, fire away . . . uh-huh, uh-huh, Oh, eviction? How do you spell that, two eff's or one? Oh, *vee,* right. Well, you learn something new every day, don't you? Yes, I'll leave it where Mr. Thorne can see, O.K. Not at all, and a good morning to you. *(Hangs up)* Where the hell is Captain Marvel!

MARTIN: You're not worried about the Arts Council, are you?

STUART: I'm beginning to be. You know what Captain Marvel's like. He's quite capable of forgetting he's meant to be at the meeting—picking up some bloody girl on the train and bundling her straight off to bed to some hotel—

MARTIN: Yes, but never when he's had to be somewhere important.

STUART: He's never had to be anywhere important before. Besides, the fact is I don't trust him to explain the value of all the stuff I gave him—when I pointed out Hubert's poems, do you know what he said? "Oh, right," and

25

shoved them into that appalling calfskin briefcase of his.
"Oh, right."

MARTIN: I don't see that that matters. I mean, that he
doesn't appreciate Hubert Stout's poetry—or any of the
other stuff you gave him, if it comes to that. Just think of
the way he got his first lectureship at Oxford. Before he'd
even published his first book.

STUART: His only chance of getting the lectureship was *before* he'd published that book.

MARTIN: That's exactly what I mean. He's a born hustler,
and that's exactly what you need at the Arts Council.
And that's why you chose him in the first place, remember? So stop worrying.

STUART: Right. Thank you. But do you mind if I worry
just a little. Until he actually arrives here with the news?
As my whole future depends upon it. *(Smiles at* MARTIN*)*

MARTIN *(Smiles back):* All right. Just a little. How's Marigold?

STUART: Oh, she's fine. A bit preoccupied at the moment. I
think the teaching's getting her down.

MARTIN: Oh. And who's the girl with the Welsh accent?

STUART: I don't know. Who is she?

MARTIN: I don't know either. But when I phoned you at
your flat last night, I got a girl with a Welsh accent. Very

26

nice and talkative, but all she seemed to know was that you'd moved out and—Marigold had gone away somewhere.

STUART: Oh yes. She's gone to Tunbridge Wells for a few days. To visit her parents. One of them is ill. She's due back this morning.

MARTIN: Her parents?

STUART: Yes.

MARTIN: But I thought she only had a father.

STUART: That's right. Then that must be the one who's ill. I didn't get along with her mother either, especially when she was alive.

MARTIN: Ah. *(Nods. Little pause)* But then who was the girl with the Welsh accent?

STUART: That must have been her flatmate.

MARTIN: Oh. But I thought—well, *(Little laugh)* that *you* were her flatmate.

STUART: Of course I am. It's just that last week we discovered that neither of us could afford my share of the rent. So I moved out, and Marigold got a teacher from her school to move in. She wanted somewhere temporary to stay. I didn't notice the Welsh accent.

MARTIN: Where are you living, then?

27

STUART: Here, of course.

MARTIN: Here? *(Looks around)* But what do you sleep on?

STUART: On the floor. There's a sleeping bag in the cupboard.

MARTIN: But what—well, what do you do about washing, and all that?

STUART: Slip into the Greek place around the corner. They've seen me around so often they think I'm one of the waiters. By the way, I shouldn't eat there if I were you. The lavatory's virtually attached to the oven.

MARTIN: But why on earth don't you come and stay with me? You can have either of the spare rooms. Or both of them. I can move old Samantha back to my bed. Where she longs to be anyway, and would be, if she didn't make me sneeze. So why don't you move in? Tonight, if you want.

STUART: Thanks. But I'm here from strategy too, you see. I have an odd feeling. To do with territory. That after seven years it would be harder to get me out of here if I've made this completely mine at last. If Giorgio does try to evict me, he'll get nervous if he finds I'm sleeping here. He'll start imagining me as some animal defending his lair. A threatened lion or a trapped tiger. Or a bankrupt rat. Anyway, something savage with teeth and jaws.

MARTIN: You know, the awful thing is, I just couldn't live like you. I'd love to be able to, but I actually couldn't.

28

STUART: Oh, it's actually quite easy. All it takes is no money.

(Pause)

MARTIN: Oh, by the way, I haven't told you yet, have I? I'm thinking of quitting.

STUART: Quitting what?

MARTIN: My job, of course, at Haylife and Forling.

STUART: Really? Why? I thought you were doing better and better there.

MARTIN: Yes, but the trouble is the books we publish are getting worse and worse. You should see this month's list. Even the titles are ungrammatical.

STUART: Does that matter? They're books for people who can't read anyway. You know, he should have been here —or at least phoned—a good, what?—twenty minutes ago.

MARTIN: Actually, I've already made some plans. I'd like to discuss them with you.

STUART: Really, what?

(Telephone rings STUART *looks at it despairingly)*

MARTIN: I'll take it. *(Answering, with Irish accent)* Hello. *The Common Pursuit. (In his normal voice)* Oh, hello,

Erika. *(Winces at* STUART) No, it's not Stuart, it's Martin. Do you want Peter? He hasn't turned up yet, I'm afraid. Oh, you want me, do you, how nice. What can I do for you? *(Pause)* What time precisely am I meeting him? I was just saying to Stuart, I wasn't quite sure. Ah, one-thirty at L'Epicure. Don't worry, I'll be there. No, no, I haven't forgotten. *Sex Scandals,* that's right. *(Pause)* Curtain rods. Right. Got that. See you soon, Erika. I've really got to go now if I'm going to make it on time. Goodbye. *(Hangs up)* This time, so the Ghastly Erika tells me, I'm having lunch with Peter to discuss a book I've commissioned from him called *Sex Scandals in Nineteenth-Century Politics.* I'm to remind him not to forget the curtain rods.

STUART: What do you mean?

MARTIN: Nothing. He's simply using me as an alibi. He does it all the time. I wish he'd warn me.

STUART: An alibi. What for?

MARTIN: Why, for coming up to London, of course.

STUART: He has forgotten.

MARTIN: What . . . ?

STUART: The meeting, he's forgotten the meeting.

MARTIN: How does that follow . . . ?

30

STUART: Because if he'd remembered the meeting he wouldn't need an alibi, would he? He already had a perfectly good reason for coming to London. I'd like to kill him. Yes. Kill him.

MARTIN: I should have told Erika the truth. She'd kill him for us.

STUART: You know what this means, don't you? Without the grant I'll have to cancel the next issue too. Making it three in a row and then go back to the usual round of begging, borrowing, and stealing; and I'll have to return Hubert's poems. He won't let me hold on to them indefinitely. So. My special place in literary history is likely to be as the editor of a small literary magazine, who, through a combination of craft, bribery, and moral blackmail, actually got his hands on six—six!—major new poems by a major poet. And then had to send them back because as it turned out he didn't actually have a magazine to publish them in. Have I got matters into perspective?

MARTIN: Well, not quite. Actually, you don't need the grant. That's what I was going to discuss with you. Just before Erika phoned. I want to offer you a partnership, Stuart.

STUART: A partnership?

MARTIN: I'm going to set up as an independent publisher. I've always had the capital; now I've got the experience. We'd be partners, you see. You would commission and edit the fiction and the poetry. I'd do the business side

31

and any editorial hackwork. I've learnt an enormous amount at Haylife and Forling's, I really have. I'm ready. *(Little pause)* And the point is, we'd keep *The Common Pursuit* going. As our subsidiary.

STUART: Subsidiary?

MARTIN: We wouldn't have to depend on the Arts Council. And I know how much you'd like that. You've always said that they only give it out so that they can take it away when it really matters.

MARTIN *(Little pause):* And you could move back with Marigold. The two of you could live, well, you know, like a couple at last. As I know you've always wanted. Especially with a baby coming.

STUART *(After a little pause):* How did you know about that??

MARTIN: Oh, well I had lunch with Marigold last week, you see. The day after she found out she was expecting.

STUART: She's not expecting. She's merely pregnant. *(Little pause)* I wonder why she didn't tell me. About your having lunch, I mean, not about being merely pregnant.

MARTIN: Actually, because I asked her not to. I wanted to know what she thought you'd feel about the prospect of coming in with me. But I didn't want to press ahead with you until I'd, well, sorted a few things out. Which I now have, actually. And was in a position to make you what they call *(Slight laugh)* a formal proposal. Which I now am. You see?

STUART: And what did she think I'd feel?

MARTIN: Oh, well, to be honest, she refused to say. All she said was that it had to be your decision.

STUART: I wonder why— *(He stops)*

MARTIN: What?

STUART: Why she told you she was pregnant. We'd agreed not to make it public. Until we'd made up our minds whether or not we wanted to have it.

MARTIN: No doubt because of Samantha.

(STUART *looks at* MARTIN)

MARTIN: She's pregnant, too. Didn't I tell you?

STUART *(Ironically):* No. Congratulations.

MARTIN *(Laughs):* Thank you. It's probably the only one I'll allow her, poor thing, before getting her fixed. She should litter in about a week. And I offered her a tabby, because she adores tabbies, as you know—Marigold, I mean. Samantha seems to adore them, too, at least the one I hope is the father. He was hanging around at the right time. A real old-fashioned Tom. A right rogue.

(There is a pause)

STUART: Oh, I see. So you and Marigold were just swapping pregnancy gossip?

MARTIN: Well, what actually happened was that I was rabbiting on in that boring way of mine when on cats, and Marigold suddenly, well, broke down and told me she was pregnant. And then asked me not to tell you she'd told me. Because of your agreement. To wait. So I'd rather you didn't tell her, if you don't mind.

STUART: Tell her that you told me that she told you? But how can I? As she only told you during a lunch you told her not to tell me you were having.

MARTIN: Quite.

(MARTIN *laughs.* STUART *smiles*)

MARTIN: Quite. So I suppose, under the circumstances I can't tell you how passionately she, well, seems to want to have the baby, can I?

STUART: Under the circumstances, no, you can't. But then you don't have to. As I know. These things tend to slip out, between long-established couples.

MARTIN *(Nods):* Sorry. *(Little pause)* Well then. What do you think? About our setting up as partners in publishing. Keeping *The Common Pursuit* going?

STUART: Yes, well, thanks. *Really* thanks, Martin. But I'd rather keep the magazine independent. I've always believed that editing it is a full-time job. Even when it's failing to appear. I haven't forgotten that I owe you quite a lot of money, by the way.

MARTIN: The money was a gift to *The Common Pursuit*. You know how much I want it to survive.

STUART: Yes I do. So do I. Want it to survive. But not as a subsidiary to something else, you see. It has to come first.

MARTIN: Before Marigold and the baby? Stuart, it'll break her heart not to have it.

(HUMPHRY *enters*)

HUMPHRY *(Enters):* Hello, what's going on? This room reeks of passion, in a famous phrase. What have you two been up to?

MARTIN: Nothing. We're waiting for Peter.

STUART: Although we suspect he's forgotten to come.

HUMPHRY: Oh. He'll turn up. Is this all there is? *(Surveying the opened wine bottles)*

MARTIN: No, there's some there.

STUART: What makes you say that?

HUMPHRY: What?

STUART: That he'll turn up.

35

HUMPHRY: Because I saw him only two days ago when I went to give a paper at Oxford. I had dinner with him. And Ghastly Erika. And their babies. He boasted that he was coming down here this morning to do what he called your street-fighting for you. Why do you think I'm here, if not to observe you in crisis and triumph. You're evidently handling the crisis part badly; let's hope you come up to snuff in the triumph part.

STUART: And you in the disaster part. *(To* MARTIN) Tell him.

MARTIN: Well, there's a possibility that Peter's coming to London for one of his usual——um——

STUART: Fucks.

HUMPHRY: Of course he is. He'd go anywhere and do anything for a fuck. Including even attending an Arts Council meeting on your behalf.

MARTIN: Yes, but you see——he lied to Erika about why he was coming up to London. He told her he was coming to see me to discuss a book, which isn't true, instead of saying he was going to the meeting, which would have been true, and the obvious lie to tell, because at least it would have been true, if he remembered it. If you follow.

HUMPHRY: Of course I follow. Merely because you can't speak properly doesn't mean I can't understand you. Generally well before you're finished. I suppose you got all this from Erika?

36

*Ellen Parker and William Converse-Roberts in the
American premiere at the Long Wharf Theatre.*

Peter Friedman, Mark Arnott, Nathan Lane and Michael Countryman in the American premiere production.

Nathan Lane and Michael Countryman in the American premiere production.

Peter Friedman and William Converse-Roberts in the American premiere production.

*Peter Friedman, Nathan Lane and Michael Countryman
in the American premiere production.*

MARTIN: Well, not about coming for the fuck.

HUMPHRY: The reason he lied to Erika was that it was simpler and less fatiguing than telling her the truth. Have you tried talking to that woman recently? A simple statement from you is followed by an imbecile question from her, and she doesn't stop until your statements have become as imbecile as her questions, in a ghastly parody of a Socratic dialogue. Then, as you sit drained of ideas, energy, humanity, she changes a baby in front of you. Virtually all over you, in fact. He had absolutely no right to marry her. Getting her pregnant was no excuse. We should have talked Nick into taking his place. He's got nothing particularly important to do with his life, and they'd have got on perfectly. Her pathological need to ask imbecile questions would actually give a purpose to his pathological need to tell lies. *(To* MARTIN*)* Do you follow?

MARTIN: I think so.

HUMPHRY: Explain it back to me, then.

MARTIN: It was easier to tell Erika he was coming to see me to discuss a book than to explain about the Arts Council, the magazine, grants, et cetera, and Stuart.

HUMPHRY: Exactly. Furthermore he won't let you down because *a)* he's a good and loyal friend, *b)* he actually longs to crusade on Stuart's behalf because, *c)* he's got nothing better to do with his life either. And he's only twenty-eight. Unlike Nick he actually had a mind, a few years back. What'll he be like when he's forty? Probably exactly the same only less so, having less energy to be it with.

MARTIN: Yes.

STUART: What?

MARTIN: I think Humphry's got it right as usual.

STUART: Then why isn't he here? He's now actually late. Or why hasn't he phoned?

HUMPHRY: Wait, thou child of hope. For time shall give thee all things. Except a decent glass of wine, at least here. Ever. This is simultaneously bland and acid—is it English?

MARTIN: Of course not, it's French. It's a chablis. *(Checks label)* A vintage in fact, isn't it? At least that's what they told me.

HUMPHRY *(Going to shelf, pours himself stale wine)*: How's Marigold? Still teaching at that school?

STUART *(Little pause, making an effort)*: Fine, she's taken a few days off. To go down to Tunbridge Wells to visit her mother. Who's ill.

MARTIN: Her father.

STUART: Yes. That's right. Her father.

38

HUMPHRY: Odd how Martin always seems to know more about your life than you do. *(To* STUART*)* Perhaps because he takes a greater interest. Anyway, you're all right, are you, you two?

STUART: Which two?

HUMPHRY: You and Marigold.

STUART: Why do you ask?

HUMPHRY: Because when I phoned you at your flat last night I got an exceptionally loquacious Indian girl, from the sound of her. She gave the distinct impression that you and Marigold were no longer living together. Although I can't be sure. Her rhythms got in the way of her sense.

STUART *(After a pause):* As a matter of fact she's pregnant. And we're going to get married.

(MARTIN *looks at him*)

HUMPHRY *(After a little pause):* Good.

STUART: Really? You don't think we have a duty to talk me out of it? Or get Nick to take my place?

HUMPRHY *(He looks at* STUART*):* I've got the greatest admiration for Marigold, as you know.

STUART: Why? Because she's got a fine mind?

39

HUMPHRY: No, she hasn't. But when it comes to the things that matter, she's got a mind of her own, which is more important. Congratulations.

(STUART *nods*)

HUMPHRY: And now to a vastly more passionate relationship. *(To* MARTIN) How's Samantha? Kindly confine your reply to two sentences.

MARTIN: Oh, she's pregnant. But we're not going to get married. What about you?

HUMPHRY: I'm not pregnant. And I wouldn't dream of getting married, even if I were. My only news is that I've changed my accommodation at last. I've moved into Great Court. Your old rooms as a matter of fact, Stuart. I've always wanted them, did you know that? But that ridiculous Northerner who lived above you took them over when he got his fellowship, and so I'd given up hope. But last month he committed suicide.

MARTIN: Oh Christ.

HUMPHRY: Quite upsetting, isn't it? I mean people we convert into jokes have an obligation not to do that sort of thing. He was a mathematical genius apparently, but his creative juices dried up suddenly. As they tend to with mathematicians. They finish young. Actually he must have been rather short on real personality, in spite of his bluster, as he hasn't left the trace of a ghost behind. Even in the bedroom, where he did it with a razor. I haven't even bothered to have it redecorated. The odd thing is that I feel I'm finally where I always intended to be. At home, in other words. So much so that this morning I rose at six, walked twice round Great Court, and wrote the first fourteen and a half lines of my book on Wagner.

MARTIN: That's marvelous, Humpty.

(The door opens. NICK *enters, coughing, with cigarette in his mouth)*

NICK: That does it. *(Coughing)* I'm giving up taxis. The way that shit of a driver took the corners, my bum skidding, my stomach churning, my head pounding, God I wish I'd thrown up. All over the back of his neck. It was red, with ginger hair on it.

MARTIN: Where were you coming from?

NICK: Don't know. Earls Court, it looked like. Some girl picked me up at a publishing party last night, took me back to her place. At least I hope it was a girl. Had her back to me when I woke up. Had a girl's spine. Smelt like a girl. But snoring like a man. So it was either an Australian or a hermaphrodite or both. The haunting question is whether I poked it, I keep recalling a brief spasm during the night. I hope it was just my cough. News from Captain Marvel?

MARTIN: We're waiting.

NICK: Oh, well I've only a few minutes—but don't worry. The grant's in the bag.

HUMPHRY: Nicholas's confidence is the first real alarm signal.

NICK: Hey, Humpty, what's all this I've been hearing? About you.

HUMPHRY: What have you been hearing?

NICK: About your lethal effect on the Cambridge undergraduate sensibility, and— *(Seeing something on* HUMPHRY's *face, changing tack)* other tittle-tattle, very complimentary about you as an intellectual glamor figure because of your lectures and stuff, from Harrop. Nappies Harrop. He was at the party too. The little creep is everywhere these days. Private viewings, first nights, publishing binges, wherever I go. Nappies is already there, standing in a corner, shoulders hunched, light gleaming off his bald pate, boasting shyly about his latest triumph, and do you know what he claims? He claims his latest, latest triumph is that he's won the Cheltenham Prize. For that nappy full of homosexless verse he dropped last year.

MARTIN: Well, he has, hasn't he?

NICK: How do you know? He told me he wasn't allowed to tell anyone until the announcement.

MARTIN: Stuart was one of the judges.

STUART: In fact I voted for him.

NICK: You didn't tell me.

STUART: No, well I'm not allowed to tell anyone either.

NICK: But how could you vote for Nappies? You know I loathe him.

STUART: I didn't vote for him. I voted for his poems.

NICK: God, Stuart, how could you be so frivolous?

STUART: Why are you so sure the grant's in the bag?

NICK: Because Captain Marvel told me so himself.

STUART: When?

NICK: Last night. He phoned to say he was coming to London for the meeting, what about lunch afterwards, along with the rest of us, but I can't make it because I'm having lunch with *Vogue.*

MARTIN: *Vogue?*

NICK: Um, uh, yes, to discuss doing a series of articles on this and that, but he said, en passant, the grant was in the bag. *(He coughs violently)*

HUMPHRY: That's aesthetically one of the least attractive ways of killing yourself, Nicholas, why don't you stop it?

NICK: Yes. Well, I will. I've got to go. Love to Captain Marvel, sorry I missed him— Oh, Martin, I think I'd better not take one of your kittens after all. For one thing they turn into cats, and I'm less soppy about those and also I'm too young to settle down. Well, see you soon, everyone. *(He goes to the door and stops)* Oh God, I almost forgot, Stuart. *Snakes and Ladders.*

STUART: What?

NICK: My article. *Snakes and Ladders.*

STUART: Ah, yes. Well, the fact is I haven't had a chance to read it properly yet. I've looked at it of course, but I haven't— *(He gestures)*

NICK: No, that's all right, but can I have it back for a while?

STUART: Certainly.

NICK: I'm not really happy with some sections of it, especially the couple of pages on Angela Thark, for instance. I didn't know she was dying when I wrote it, don't forget. I'd like to be more—more delicate. Cut out the bit about her menstrual obsession, her blood-soaked prose, etc., and get at some of the reviewers for not admiring her more—she's got that daughter, after all. Grieving friends. I'm one myself, in a way.

(STUART has gone to his desk and is looking for the manuscript)

MARTIN: I thought you couldn't stand her.

NICK: Death brings its own respect. *(He gives a little laugh)* And I always maintained that she was sexy. Anyway, the point is I can't let the article go as it stands. It makes me seem a brute. Which I am, about her. But I can't afford to seem it, can I?

STUART *(Still looking):* I can't find it. Can you work from your own copy?

NICK: No, I can't. I destroyed it. I lost a bit of confidence in it, you see, when you went off failing to mention it every time I saw you. Not that I'm blaming you. I destroyed a lot of other stuff too. Virtually my whole life's work. Threw it all in the fire, as a matter of fact. I sometimes wonder whether you realize what an influence you have, Stuart. You've always been the reader over our shoulder. Hasn't he? Any luck?

STUART: It's here somewhere.

NICK *(Conscious that* HUMPHRY *is watching him):* You know, I'm beginning to wonder whether I'm really cut out for a career in literature. I find writing even more of a chore than fucking. And a lot of the people one meets are even worse. Actually, I wish I were a simple rural vicar. Riding about among my parishioners on a bike, with my dog running behind my rear wheel, my wife at home with the children. And with a little bit of faith to keep me going. Oh, and a private income too. Two private incomes. *(Laughs, avoiding* HUMPHRY's *eye. To* STUART) Any luck?

HUMPHRY: What I can't work out is why?

NICK: Why what?

HUMPHRY: Why you're lying, Nicholas. Your motive. Or are you just keeping in practice?

MARTIN: You don't think by any chance, well, he's *sold Snakes and Ladders?* To somebody else, I mean.

HUMPHRY: *Vogue,* of course!

STUART: What?

HUMPHRY: Nicholas has sold it to *Vogue.* Well done, Martin.

NICK *(Little pause):* Yes, well, actually what happened is that I sent a copy to my agent.

HUMPHRY: The ashes of your copy, you mean. You burnt it, remember, along with the rest of your life's work.

NICK: Yes, well— *(Gestures)* and she showed it to *Vogue,* without my consent naturally, and it turned out that *Vogue* was thinking of doing a piece along those lines. So they snapped it up.

STUART: And that's why you want my copy back, is it? Nothing to do with Angela Thark at all.

NICK: Well, my agent says she doesn't like the thought of it being offered to two different magazines at the same time. She says it's unethical. And I agree with her.

(STUART, MARTIN, *and* HUMPHRY *laugh*)

46

NICK: Perhaps. But bloody hell, I'm a professional literary journalist. I live by what I sell. And you didn't bother to acknowledge receiving it, let alone let me know what you thought about it. Do you realize it's six years since you last asked me to contribute something—and the fact is, it could lie rotting away on your desk forever. The magazine's failed to come out twice running now, and there's a decent chance it'll never come out again.

(Pause)

STUART: A decent chance, is it?

NICK: According to Peter.

STUART: According to Peter when?

NICK: This morning. He stopped in for a cup of coffee on his way to the meeting.

STUART: But you were coming from an Australian or a hermaphrodite in Earls Court this morning.

HUMPHRY: Whom you either poked or coughed into.

NICK: Ahhh . . . ! Yes. Well, that must have been yesterday morning. In fact, it sounds like all my yesterday mornings recently. Except tomorrow. Because tomorrow I'll have had coffee with Peter yesterday. Won't I? *(He attempts a laugh, coughs instead)*

STUART: And what precisely did he say? About the grant?

47

NICK: Yes, well—apparently the whole Arts council panel, virtually, thinks you're elitist.

STUART: Elitist.

NICK: He's going to do his best, but he reckons you haven't got a chance. But knowing you, you'll struggle on for years, editing a magazine that never comes out at all. And I'll have missed the opportunity of getting in with *Vogue.* And I need it. Can I have the article, please?

STUART: Actually no, you can't. I must have accidentally stuck it in with the material I gave Captain Marvel to show the Arts Council. So it was probably sitting in his briefcase when you had coffee with him. But don't worry, Nick, I shan't publish it. The truth is I've been wondering how to return it to you without hurting you. All you had to do was to say straight out that *Vogue* wanted it, did I mind. I'd have been delighted. It's perfect for *Vogue.* Just as it stands. But I don't think it could ever be good enough for *The Common Pursuit.*

NICK: Yes—well, they're right. You *are* elitist.

STUART: Well, somebody's got to be, haven't they? Especially at a time when nobody else wants to be.

NICK: But they don't want you to be either. Do they? They're not interested in your high critical standards and intellectual rigor and traditional poetic forms—in fact, they don't want *The Common Pursuit.* The magazine's finished, Stuart. Why don't you face it and come out into the real world at last?

HUMPHRY: Where is the real world, Nicholas? Somewhere among the lingerie and perfume ads in *Vogue?*

NICK: Yes, well, you're exactly like Stuart, aren't you, Humpty? You can't face the facts about yourself either.

(There is a pause)

HUMPHRY: Well, go on, Nick. Help me face the facts about myself. Say them to me. The facts.

(NICK *stares at* HUMPHRY. MARIGOLD *enters)*

MARIGOLD: Hello, chaps.

MARTIN: Marigold.

HUMPHRY: Marigold.

MARIGOLD: Hello, Humpty. I didn't know you were coming down.

NICK: Hi, Marigold.

MARIGOLD: Nicholas.

MARTIN: How's your mother?

MARIGOLD: My mother? She's been dead for four years.

MARTIN: I'm terribly sorry—I meant your father of course.

MARIGOLD: They've discovered he's got a bad heart. So he'll have to give up all the things he really lives for: Scotch, cigarettes, and his furtive little forays up to the dirty bookshops. To balance that, he's got to give up his job too, but he won't mind that, as he's always hated it.

NICK: He's a doctor, isn't he?

MARIGOLD: No, a vicar.

HUMPHRY: Oh. Then, Nicholas, you should meet him. Nicholas was just saying a moment ago he was thinking of going into the church—weren't you, Nicholas? He has some of the right qualifications. He lies badly about things that don't matter.

MARIGOLD: What have you been up to this time?

HUMPHRY: Come on, Nicholas, tell her.

NICK: I'm sorry— *(Kisses* MARIGOLD's *hand)* —I've got to go, I'm late. See you all then. *(He goes to the door, hesitates)* Look. *(To* STUART) I'm—sorry. *(Coughs slightly, goes out)*

MARIGOLD: What's he done?

STUART: Merely withdrawn his unwanted article on inconsequential literary figures of our time.

MARIGOLD: But that's good, isn't it? You were agonizing over how to tell him.

50

STUART: It was the way he did it, Nick being Nick.

HUMPHRY: Of course you realize he only offered the article to *Vogue* to spare himself the humiliation of your rejecting it. Which he nevertheless has just managed to achieve, Nicholas being Nicholas. Good to hear about the baby, but that doesn't mean you have to marry him, you know.

MARIGOLD *(Laughs):* Thank you. *(Looks at STUART)*

STUART: I decided to make it official. As word seems to be getting round anyway. *(Looks at MARTIN)*

MARIGOLD: Ah. *(Also glances at MARTIN)* But where's our Captain Marvel? I thought he was meant to be here by now?

STUART: We think he may not make it, but it doesn't matter, as he sent a message via Nick. We're not getting our grant. On the grounds that we're elitist.

MARIGOLD *(After a little pause):* Elitist?

STUART: All right, let's face it, or rather let me face it, at least. It's probably the right decision. The fact is that *The Common Pursuit* doesn't really matter, to anyone except me. As Nick pointed out. *(Little laugh)* To do him credit.

MARIGOLD *(To STUART):* You're not seriously talking of giving up! Not now! You can't. He can't, can he?

STUART: Oh, yes I can.

51

MARIGOLD: But—but it's not fair. *(She gives a little laugh)* After eight years, it's actually not fair.

STUART: Oh yes it is. The printers want their money, and why shouldn't they have it? They've worked hard for it. Giorgio wants his rent, and why shouldn't he have it? He owns the place. I can't pay the telephone bill, the electricity bill; I can't even pay for the issues of the magazine I *fail* to bring out. If "fair" means anything, it's time I was fair to them. And time I was fair to you. Especially now. Come on, Humpty. Let's hear the truth.

HUMPHRY: But you've just spoken it. Almost. Even if you get the grant, you'll be having a version of this conversation a baby or two from now.

(Pause)

MARIGOLD: You don't know everything! You don't always know everything!

STUART: Yes, well, trust Humpty to go the unpalatable stage further. But he is right. In the end the magazine won't survive.

MARIGOLD *(To* HUMPHRY *and* MARTIN): Can I—look, do you mind if I talk to Stuart?

MARTIN: I'm sorry. I didn't mean to. It just—just slipped out. I'm sorry. *(Exits)*

(HUMPHRY *goes to* MARIGOLD, *bends down, kisses her)*

MARIGOLD *(With a little laugh, hugs him):* Oh, Humpty. I'm sorry.

(HUMPHRY *goes out. There is a pause)*

MARIGOLD: You're doing it because of the baby, aren't you?

STUART: No, I'm not.

MARIGOLD: I don't believe you. What would you have done if there hadn't been a baby? You'd have gone on. You know you would.

STUART: If so, it would have been out of habit.

MARIGOLD: Look—you've talked about facts. Well, you're the only fact in my life. You know you are. From the first moment we started, you and the magazine came together. And the magazine has always been a part of your life. I've not just accepted that, it's how I want things to be. How I want you to be. To go on being. You won't be you without it. Oh, please, my love—please. You mustn't give up. You mustn't.

STUART: I've got to give up. I don't want *The Common Pursuit* anymore. It's already in the past. Look, when I found myself announcing to Humphry that you were pregnant and that we were going to get married, well, my heart turned over. It was joy. And after that things began —simply to drop away. So that by the time you came into the room, I found myself gazing on the central . . . well, fact in my life. Not the magazine. You. Us. It always has been. I've merely behaved as if it were the other way

53

around. Now I see it so clearly I want to start again. From there.

MARIGOLD: I've had an abortion.

(STUART *stares at her*)

MARIGOLD: I didn't go to see my father. I didn't want you to have to choose—I knew we couldn't cope, even if you got the grant. (*Looks at* STUART) Please don't say any-thing. Help me. Please.

(PETER *bursts into the room, carrying a calfskin briefcase in one hand, curtain rods in the other*)

PETER: Sorry I'm late. Had to stop off to buy some bloody curtain rods, can you believe it, I promised Erika. (*Putting stuff down, turns*) Anyway, SHAZAM! I've got your grant. In spades! They've undertaken to guarantee all your costs, clear all your outstanding debts, pay your rent, and provide you with a salary that will lift you at least into our lowest income tax bracket, plus bona fide expenses for the odd literary binge for African poets in transit and so forth. Which is, I think, substantially more than you expected and more than substantially more than I thought we had a hope in hell of getting, which was frankly nothing. But I did it all on my silver tongue and contents of my briefcase. Congratulate me!

MARIGOLD: Oh, Peter, you've done wonderfully. Thank you! Thank you!

PETER: Oh, I know it's not enough to live and breed on, but going by my own experience, who wants to do that? *(Laughs)* But a bit of credit to old Nick too, eh?

STUART: Nick?

PETER: They're such shits! The only thing those salaried buggers with pensions to come know about you is that you are elitist. So that was that—nothing to discuss. Until I read out Nick's article. To tell you the truth I didn't even know it was there. It just happened to be the first thing I plucked out of my briefcase, a despairing gesture, really, while I shouted angrily at them about how could they ignore the value and quality, et cetera, of this sort of thing, and one of them said, "Well, read it out then. Let's judge it on its merits, shall we?" So I had to, of course. When I realized it was by Nick, and knew the kind of stuff that was coming, I nearly threw up, and Christ it was awful, so of course they loved it. All his appalling jokes about Angela Thark and menstruation had them falling about. They wanted more samples of what you planned for the future, so I pulled out a sheaf of poems. That clinched it.

STUART: Hubert's.

PETER: No, those Belfast hooligans, Leary and O'— O'—

STUART: Dougan. Though actually it's Dougan and O'Leary.

PETER: Yes. They adored them for their directness, their simplicity, their brutal rhymes and vocabulary, their— their singsong—

STUART: Lack of talent. They were in the wrong bundle, too. I was going to send them back.

PETER: You mustn't. That poem about shit exploding in our faces made up for all the Hubert Stouts. Which they loathed on the grounds that they were—were—

STUART: Poems.

PETER: Exactly. What were they about? Must say, I couldn't make much of them either. Perhaps teaching in Oxford has addled my brain, eh? Anyway, the thing is— you're off and running.

STUART: Peter, thank you.

PETER: No, I enjoyed it. I mean, what could be nicer than paying out large sums of taxpayers' money to one's chums. *(To* MARIGOLD*)* But God you look ravishing— And I haven't kissed you yet— *(Does so)* —but distraught. Are you distraught?

MARIGOLD: No, perfectly traught, thanks.

PETER: Terrific! Oh, do you mind if I use the phone? *(Goes to telephone)* Somebody's waiting on my call. Oh, by the way, Humpty was up in Oxford the other evening, to give a paper, a very short one I heard afterwards, but he came over for dinner *(Looking for a phone number on scraps of paper taken from his pockets)* very relaxed and charming, anyway, for Humpty. But then Erika always brings out the best in him; they seem to have a rapport, partly because she doesn't think much of his intellect, just goes on being herself, gets him to help with the children, changes the baby, that sort of thing, he loves it really—ah, here we are! *(Finding number)* Oh, by the way, who is that in your flat, is she foreign or what?

MARIGOLD: Yes, she's from Manchester.

PETER: Manchester? Really? Sounded like an Arab to me. *(Into phone)* Joan, hello! What, yes I know, that's what I said, Jean, so hello, Jean. Sorry, I'm running a bit late, I've just been pulling some chestnuts out of the fire for an old friend. What? Oh, I'm phoning from his office. *Of course* I'm alone! Anyway, look, I've booked us into the Charing Cross Hotel. *(Little pause)* Because they know me there, it'll be a good room, we'll have postcoital views of the Strand, eh? So I'll see you in the bar in— *(Checks watch)*—in eight and a half minutes. Oh—and why don't you bring the um—you know. Right. See you, um, darling. *(Hangs up)* Oh, has Erika phoned?

STUART: Yes.

PETER: What did she want?

STUART: To remind you to get the curtain rods.

PETER: Oh yes. Well, if she phones again, remind her of my arrangement to meet Martin about the book on—um—

STUART: *Sex Scandals in Nineteenth-Century Politics.*

PETER: Yes. And then tell her I'll be going on to Selfridges to pick up the curtain rods, and then I'm meeting Nick and Humpty for a drink, and then I'm having dinner with you two, and I'll be back on the last train, but that I won't be able to call her probably because of the bloody disgraceful condition of the telephone boxes in London, but that she's not to worry, all my love. Right? What they call tit for tat. Not that *The Common Pursuit*'s tat. *(Laughs)* But I'm after tit! *(Exits, with briefcase, without curtain rods)*

(Pause. STUART *walks around, touching various objects in the room. Spots the curtain rods)*

STUART: He's forgotten them. The curtain rods.

MARIGOLD: So he has. *(There is a pause)* So I've been saved, then, haven't I? Just in the nick of time. So perhaps there is a God after all.

STUART: You mean the Arts Council? More like a devil, I suspect. *(Turns around, smiles at her)* I'm not tempted.

MARIGOLD *(After a small pause):* You're not going to accept the grant, then?

STUART: Of course not.

MARIGOLD: No. *(In despair)* Oh why—why are you so obstinate?

Act One

STUART: I've told you already. I love you. We're going to get married. And have babies. Lots of babies. All the babies you want. And more.

MARIGOLD: Oh, my love.

(Lights)

CURTAIN

ACT TWO

ACT II

SCENE 1

STUART's and MARTIN's office. Three years later. Late afternoon.

The office is transformed, painted and orderly. STUART still has the same desk, in the same position. Opposite is MARTIN's desk, slightly smaller than STUART's, but more antique. On both desks, a telephone. There is also a desk in the corner with a typewriter on it, a vase of flowers, some photographs propped, a secretarial desk. On the walls there are some bookshelves, but now full of books, most of them evidently proofs of coffee-table style books. On the walls, covers of books on gardening, nursing, cricket, bridge, Napoleon, Hitler, Churchill, etc., some by Peter Whetworth, and a poster for the poetry reading, new, by Dougan and O'Leary.

There is a new armchair, a new sofa, a couple of hard-backed chairs, and an elegant and antique cocktail cabinet. On MARTIN's desk, and on the wall above his desk are photographs, drawings, cartoons, and reproductions of paintings of cats.

The sound of footsteps on the stairs. MARTIN increases the speed of his typing as HUMPHRY enters. He is carrying an overnight bag. He looks around, has trouble locating MARTIN in the corner as MARTIN types.

MARTIN: Hi, Humpty. Won't be a second. (Scribbling his signature at the bottom of the sheet)

63

HUMPHRY: Oh. Now you're being the secretary too, are you? Where's that girl of yours—what's her name, Michelle?

MARTIN: Tonight's her evening class, so I let her go home early. She has to finish her essay on *Macbeth*. Actually I expect we'll have to replace our Michelle soon. She's determined to go to university.

HUMPHRY: By far the best place for her. She's not bright enough to be a secretary.

MARTIN *(Laughs):* Want a drink?

HUMPHRY: A small brandy, to settle the stomach. It always tends to be a bit queasy after lunch with Nick.

MARTIN *(Going to the cocktail cabinet):* I've only got a classical French one, I'm afraid. Will that do? *(Extracting the bottle, pouring)* What's he up to, we haven't seen him for a few weeks, old Nick.

HUMPHRY: You might see him later. He said he'd look in. But only if he gets his television job.

MARTIN: What television job?

HUMPHRY: Presenting the new books program.

MARTIN: The one on the BBC?

HUMPHRY: So I gather.

MARTIN: Good God! You mean Nick might get that program? Nick!

HUMPHRY: Might, but lots of competition, from what he says. He's particularly worried about the current front-runner. The balding, portly poet, the one he calls Nappies.

MARTIN: Oh, Harrop. He's becoming quite famous—I've never understood why Nick hates him so much.

HUMPHRY: Because they're soul mates of course. Which is why Nick will kill him if he gets the job. I keep expecting you to move office. Aren't you getting cramped?

MARTIN: Well, frankly, yes. But Stuart's very attached to the place. But now that old Giorgio, the landlord, has died, we're probably going to have to move anyway.

HUMPHRY: Where is Stuart?

MARTIN: At the printers. We take it in turns. He hates going, but he insists on doing his stint.

HUMPHRY: Ah. And how's Marigold?

MARTIN: Oh, she's applied to be assistant head mistress at her school. We're just waiting to hear whether she's got the job. The interview's this afternoon. Where are you off to by the way?

HUMPHRY: Oh, Edinburgh. To see my parents.

MARTIN: They're still in decent fettle, I hope?

HUMPHRY: It's my father's seventy-fifth birthday tomorrow, but he's O.K. Thank you. And I've brought along a sweater I cut a hole in for my mother to darn. So she'll be O.K. too. I've also brought along a book inscribed to me by Edwina McClusky, on Plato, which they won't understand, which is just as well, as it's mainly wrong. But it'll support my boast that Edwina and I are having an affair.

MARTIN: But surely she's getting on a bit, isn't she, Edwina McCluskey?

HUMPHRY: She's seventy-four, but my parents don't know that. And I hope they don't find out or they'll think there's something wrong with me. All they suspect is that she's an older woman. Which worries them a little. Which is exactly the right amount, for parents of their age, with a son of my type. And they'll be reassured by the news that I've been appointed the college's senior moral tutor. Did we ever bump into one of those in our day? Apparently their job was to advise us on all our little problems, financial and especially emotional. A sort of uncle figure, with a cutting edge. I'm certainly the first senior moral tutor I've ever come across.

MARTIN: But you'll enjoy it, won't you?

HUMPHRY: I'm afraid I probably will. Well, Martin?

MARTIN: How's the brandy?

66

HUMPHRY: I hadn't noticed. Probably a good sign. Come on then. What do you want?

MARTIN: Why do you think I want something?

HUMPHRY: Because when you phoned to ask when I was next coming down, and I said today, you said good, please come and see us. But you and I don't usually end up in the same room unless Stuart's present, do we? And as you *didn't* say Stuart wouldn't be here, it must be something you want, and don't want Stuart to know about. Is it?

MARTIN: I sometimes wonder whether you enjoy knowing so much. Yes. Have you committed your book on Wagner to a publisher yet?

HUMPHRY: No.

MARTIN: Would you commit it to me?

HUMPHRY: To make up one of your coffee-table specials. A short and breezy life padded out with photographs and facsimiles? The sort that Captain Marvel hacks out for you? *(Looking at* PETER's *book jackets on wall)*

MARTIN *(Laughs):* I thought you'd say that. *(Small pause)* Actually I was hoping you'd do me the honor of being our first real book. A book of scholarship, judgment, and imagination. As we all know it will be. To usher in our next phase. It can be as long as you like, have no illustrations at all, if you prefer. Two, three, even four volumes. Three anyway. *(He laughs)*

67

HUMPHRY: Have you discussed this with Stuart?

MARTIN: No.

HUMPHRY: Why not?

MARTIN: Because I want it to be a surprise. He'd be your editor, you see. Would you like that?

HUMPHRY: Yes.

MARTIN: Good! Then we'll draw up a contract.

HUMPHRY: No, we won't. The slight catch, from all our points of view, is that I'm not writing a book on Wagner. I abandoned it about three weeks ago, if October the seventeenth, at three in the morning, was about three weeks ago.

MARTIN: But why, Humpty? The last time I was in Cambridge I saw how much you'd done. There was what? Three hundred pages already on your desk.

HUMPHRY: You counted them, did you, while I was out of the room?

MARTIN: Oh, come on, Humpty. I'm a professional publisher. I could see at a glance how much you'd done. You mustn't give it up. You mustn't.

HUMPHRY: Yes, I must. I've got the scholarship, and the judgment, but not the imagination. Everything I've written about him reduces him to my own sort of size. Which

68

makes him too small to be interesting to me. You see, I've discovered I have a slight flaw after all. Moral, I think, rather than intellectual. I diminish what I most admire.

MARTIN: But—well, mightn't it help if you published *something*? What about a monograph? If not on Wagner, somebody else. What about our publishing your fellowship dissertation?

HUMPHRY: It's on Hegel, Martin. In German, mostly. I stopped believing in it before I began it. I went through with it because it would allow me to work on the things I loved. Which I want to go on loving. Which is why I won't allow my intelligence to fix on them, ever again. I don't think I can be simpler, even for you.

MARTIN: I'm being selfish. I'm sorry.

HUMPHRY: You're being selfish for Stuart, as usual. I'm sorry. I expect it's all far harder for you than for me.

MARTIN *(Looks at him):* No, I'm actually very happy. *(Little pause)* Really. If that's what you mean. Although you're right, I'm sometimes not sure what you mean, being simple. *(He laughs)*

HUMPHRY: He doesn't know, then?

MARTIN: Know what?

HUMPHRY: Don't be alarmed. *(Little pause)* It's not my business.

MARTIN: Thank you.

HUMPHRY: Our lives aren't dissimilar. In spite of appearances. And reality, come to that. Can I give you some advice?

MARTIN *(Thinks):* No. Really, Humpty, thanks. I respect you far too much. I might listen to it, you see. And then I'd have nothing. Nothing I want, anyway.

(Sound of footsteps on the stairs. Coughing)

HUMPHRY: Oh Nick. He must have gotten the job. But do we want that noise on our television screens—even though it's livelier than what he'll have to say about books.

(PETER *enters*)

HUMPHRY: Peter.

PETER: Don't you ever get your bloody stairs swept? Humpty, how are you? It's been ages. Stuart not here, then?

MARTIN: No, it's his turn at the printers. I didn't know you were coming in today.

PETER: Nor did I, but I had to, as it turned out. Here you are. As promised. Two weeks of exhaustion and only a month overdue. *(Slapping a typescript down on the table)* About forty-five thousand words I worked it out at on the train, which is only fifteen thousand fewer than we

70

agreed. So if we add an extra dozen pictures—who's doing the pictures by the way? I'm looking forward to seeing what she's got.

MARTIN: Well, I think you are actually, aren't you?

PETER: Am I, bugger!

MARTIN: Yes, well that's what we usually put in the contract. Anyway, you've finished it, wonderful.

HUMPHRY: What's it on?

PETER: The great religious leaders of world history, Mohammed, Buddha, Jesus, you'll probably think I skimped a bit on Jesus, just five pages or so, as a matter of fact, but then let's face it, he's being overdone at the moment, he's always being overdone, in fact, but I'll pad him out if you think it necessary, and there's a whole chapter *(To* HUMPHRY) on Wagner, in the myth-creator section, out of deference to you. You're in the index. And the acknowledgments, Humpty.

HUMPHRY: Thank you. Why do you do it?

PETER: What?

HUMPHRY: Go on turning out books like this?

PETER: Because I've got four children. Why do you think?

MARTIN: Um, even with pictures I've got a feeling that forty-five thousand might be a trifle on the short side—

THE COMMON PURSUIT

PETER: Yes, yes, well the thing is I've got to get on up to Hamstead fairly quickly; there's somebody I've got to see. Can we go into this next time I'm here, or you and/or Stuart are in Oxford? The really crucial question is whether Erika and I can have dinner with you tonight, preferably at your place?

MARTIN: Oh, I'm sorry. Not really, I'm afraid. Not tonight.

PETER: Why not?

MARTIN: Because I'm going out to dinner.

PETER: We'll come too.

MARTIN: I'm terribly sorry. I'm afraid you can't. You see, they happen to be people I don't know. Well, I mean.

PETER: Then cancel.

MARTIN: Oh no. I couldn't do that. They're an elderly couple, you see, and they've gone to a lot of trouble. *(Little pause)* Probably a ghastly evening, but I can't let them down.

PETER: Oh Christ! Erika's made arrangements for a babysitter especially so we could have dinner with you.

MARTIN: What dinner? We never discussed any dinner.

HUMPHRY: He means you were his alibi and it's all gone wrong, at last.

72

PETER: Exactly. I told her I was having dinner with you and then I'd probably stay overnight in one of your extra rooms, as usual. But just as I was leaving she took it into her head for the first time ever—*ever*—that she wanted to come too.

(HUMPHRY *laughs slightly*)

PETER: Shut up, Humpty.

MARTIN: Well, tell her you got the day wrong. Or I did. Yes, blame me, that's the easiest.

PETER: I can't.

MARTIN: Why not?

PETER: Because she made me phone you to warn you there'd be one extra for dinner.

MARTIN: But you didn't phone me. Unless Michelle forgot to give me the message.

PETER: No, of course I didn't phone you.

(HUMPHRY *laughs again*)

PETER: Will you shut up, Humpty! No, of course I didn't phone you, but I had to pretend to. I was phoning some-body entirely different, of course.

MARTIN: Oh, who?

PETER: Jane.

MARTIN: Jane?

HUMPHRY: The girl he'd actually arranged to have dinner with, of course.

PETER: Of course. So I had to stand there trying to talk to Jane, with Erika at my elbow thinking I was talking to you, and hoping Jane would understand my saying that Erika was coming to dinner too meant that my dinner with her was off.

MARTIN: And did she?

PETER: No, because as it turned out, I wasn't talking to Jane at all. I was talking to her mother-in-law. Jane had already left Oxford. She's up in Hampstead now, still thinking we're going to have dinner.

MARTIN: Good heavens! What did she make of it?

PETER: Who?

HUMPHRY: Jane's mother-in-law.

PETER: No idea, as soon as I cottoned on to who I was actually talking to, I said, so we'll see you at eight, Erika's looking forward to it enormously, aren't you, darling, and hung up, but the thing is . . .

MARTIN: So the mother-in-law of the girl you're spending the night with in London is expecting you and Erika for dinner in Oxford. Can that be right?

PETER: Oh, don't be ridiculous, Martin, the mother-in-law hadn't the slightest idea who I was, so she doesn't know who to expect for dinner tonight, does she? So it doesn't matter. What matters is what am I going to do about Erika.

MARTIN: Why don't you phone Oxford and tell her I'm ill?

PETER: She already left. She was catching an afternoon train.

HUMPHRY: Who is Jane, exactly?

PETER: Oh, nobody. Just the wife of a friend.

MARTIN: Anyone we know?

PETER: No, no, his name's Papworth, Roland Papworth, a theologian at New College. But what—

HUMPHRY: Does he know what you're up to?

PETER: What?

HUMPHRY: Does Roland Papworth know what you're up to? With his wife, Jane.

PETER: Of course he doesn't. I wouldn't hurt old Roland for the world, he and I have become extremely close, he gave me an enormous amount of help with *Great Religious Leaders,* for one thing. He's particularly strong on Buddha. *(To* MARTIN) Can't you really get out of your dinner?

MARTIN: You don't mean he wrote it?

PETER: What?

MARTIN: This Roland Papworth, the theologian, did he write it? Your book? I need to know because of the copyright—

PETER *(Exasperated):* No, of course he didn't write it; he merely filled in a bit of the history, background, ideas, that sort of thing, and the Buddha bits, but I did most of the last draft. Of course, he's probably expecting his name on the title page; that was one of the things I wanted to discuss with you later, and he'll want a share of the royalties, but look—

MARTIN: There aren't any royalties. You get paid a fee. Half of which you've already received, you see.

PETER: Yes, well, don't worry, I'll think up some way of sharing something with him.

HUMPHRY: Apart from his wife, you mean?

PETER: What?

HUMPHRY: I suppose Jane's good in bed, is she?

PETER: Yes, well. That's not the point at the moment. The point is Erika. I don't want her to start getting suspicious after all these years.

HUMPHRY: But does that matter?

PETER *(Incredulously):* Does it matter? She'd crack up completely. We've got four bloody children. Do you think I don't care?

HUMPHRY: I know you don't care. About anything that matters.

PETER: What do you mean?

HUMPHRY: Haven't I made myself plain, even to you? That you go on spawning children and pretending to love a fatuous wife that you can't even be bothered to betray competently, while writing books on subjects that you inevitably demean.

(There is a pause. PETER *hits* HUMPHRY, *knocks him to the ground)*

PETER: What did you say that for? What did you have to say it for?

HUMPHRY *(Still on the ground):* Because I've just been made a senior moral tutor. It's our job to help people to see their little tangles more clearly.

PETER: But I've been a senior fucking moral what'sit for years. I don't go around insulting my friends and inviting them to hit me.

HUMPHRY: That's because you moved to Oxford. You've forgotten how seriously we take moral matters at Cambridge. I've got to be on my way if I'm going to just miss

77

my train, and enjoy an hour and a half hanging around the station lavatory. *(He goes to the door, turns)* I suppose I'm sorry. *(He exits. There is a pause)*

MARTIN: You all right?

PETER: Yes—yes—but I—I—why did he? That I should have hit Humpty. Of all people. Why did he?

MARTIN: I think—well, because he's so fond of you, isn't he? Fonder than of anyone else.

PETER: But I can't spend my life being what *he* needs me to be, can I?

MARTIN: No, you have to make your own life. I expect your being so prolific doesn't help either.

PETER: Yes, well that's a different matter. He'd be ashamed to have written what I've written. But then he hasn't got a family— *(He stops)* —I've got to get to Hampstead. Christ, what a day, and the worst part hasn't even begun yet. You realize what's happened, don't you?

MARTIN: You've fallen in love with, um, Jane, isn't it?

PETER *(Nods):* It's a nightmare. But Jane isn't just another —another of my fucks. I've got to get her out of my system.

MARTIN: I'm so sorry about dinner. If I could see any way.

PETER: No, I know. I had no right to involve you, really, had I? But you've been such a convenient fiction all these years. I must get going.

(STUART *enters)*

STUART: Peter.

PETER: Stuart. Hello.

STUART: I didn't know you were coming down today.

PETER: No, well, actually the pity is I'm just off. I've got to be in Hampstead—oh, Christ, ten minutes ago. I dropped in to hand over the book. I've finished it.

STUART: Terrific, Peter. That's really terrific.

PETER: There are a few complications—Martin will tell you all about them—all about everything else too, I expect. *(Little laugh)* I must really dash.

STUART: Love to Erika.

PETER: Absolutely. And to Marigold. *(Exits)*

(STUART, *clearly preoccupied, goes to his desk)*

MARTIN: Look, while I remember, Peter was desperate for me to have dinner with him and Erika for reasons too boring to go into. I told him I couldn't because I'm already going out to dinner. With an elderly couple of my acquaintance. So could you remember that if the subject ever comes up?

STUART: Right. An elderly couple. What couple?

MARTIN *(Laughs slightly):* Well, you and Marigold, of course. We're having dinner tonight, remember? And we wouldn't really want Peter and Erika tagging along, would we? Especially as Marigold will want to tell us all about her interview.

STUART: Of course.

MARTIN: You look tired. Did they give you a bad time?

STUART: Who?

MARTIN: The printers.

STUART: Yes. Well, I'm afraid I didn't go. Sorry.

MARTIN: Oh. That's all right. I can look in first thing to-morrow. *(Little pause)* Where did you go?

STUART: I went to see Hubert Stout.

MARTIN: Did he recognize you this time?

STUART: Oh, yes, straight away for once. In fact he was anxious to see me as he's written eight new poems especially for me. He's been keeping them under his mattress. He thinks the nurses or doctors will try to steal them.

80

He's decided that *The Common Pursuit* either still exists or has been born again. I don't know quite which.

MARTIN: But eight new poems. Any chance we could publish them—with an introduction by you? We might get up quite a nice little volume—well, at least a pamphlet.

STUART: Yes, but unfortunately he hasn't written eight new poems. He's written eight shopping lists, or rather the same shopping list eight times. Orders for a pound of apples, a calendar, a ball of wool, knitting needles, scissors—oh, a turvey drop.

MARTIN: What's a turvey drop?

STUART: I don't know. Anyway, the last order in his lists is for eight new poems in eight different rhyme schemes including one in terza rima. Good to know he's still experimenting with verse form. He's never worked in terza rima before.

MARTIN: Good God! What did you do?

STUART: Oh, shuffled through the bits of paper, nodding wisely until he fell asleep. Or pretended to. His eyes were shut and he made a sort of snoring noise. But there was a funny little grin under his beard, like a snarl. When I got up to go, he was clutching at my coat, it turned out. I had trouble prying myself free. I think he knew perfectly well what he'd given me. I think the trouble is he's terrified of dying. And when you think of his best poems, they're mainly about death. So urbane, so wise. Especially the ones he wrote in memory of Charlotte. So seeing him like

81

this is like a—a contamination. *(Smiles slightly)* I'd have done better to have gone to the printers.

MARTIN: Yes. Look, I know it sounds inadequate, but why don't we go somewhere special for dinner tonight? I'll book a table at L'Epicure. Marigold loves it.

STUART: Martin, I want to quit.

(MARTIN *stares at him*)

STUART: Sorry. I didn't mean to blurt it out like that.

MARTIN: But you can't quit!

STUART: Why not?

MARTIN *(Laughs):* Well—well, for one thing, you're our poetry and fiction editor. I can't manage without you.

STUART: Oh yes, you can. And we both know it. We never put out more than three novels a year and they're really just a gift from you to me. At least nobody but me seems to like them much, not enough to buy them anyway. And as for poetry, a few token volumes which I suspect nobody ever reads, let alone buys—so really just another gift from you to me. Apart, of course, from Leary and O'Dougan, Dougan and O'Leary, whose shit is still exploding in our faces, though at least at a profit. Oh, I'm not blaming you for publishing them, you're absolutely right to, but the fact is I can't face reading them, let alone editing them and that applies to almost every book we've

82

ever published, including—probably especially Captain Marvel's latest. So you see—

MARTIN: But I was going to do Peter's. I wouldn't dream of inflicting it on you. And I don't mind doing Dougan and O'Leary either. In fact, I quite like them, not as poets I mean, but they're great fun to take out to lunch. And you're quite right, the main point about them is that they're profitable. And Peter might be too, actually, come to think of it. Haven't you noticed the competition's lists? Religion's on the way back with a vengeance. People have even started killing each other again because of it. So Captain Marvel might turn out to be a blessing in disguise.

STUART: Yes, but the point is that none of that has anything to do with me.

MARTIN: No, the point is that if we go on as we have been going on for just a while longer—a year or two at the most—and then consolidate, we'll be in a position to publish the kind of book you'll be proud to edit.

STUART: Martin, I'm going to quit.

MARTIN: You should have let me keep *The Common Pursuit* going. I told you you needed it.

STUART: *The Common Pursuit* has nothing to do with it. It's me I'm talking about, as I am now—as I understand me, anyway, courtesy of Dennis.

MARTIN: Dennis? Who's Dennis?

83

STUART: The cat you gave us. Look, the other evening I was sitting in the kitchen, vaguely waiting for you and Marigold to get back from your concert. And Dennis was strutting about on the counter. Then he did one of his things. You know, he gathered himself together, eyed the top of the fridge, jumped, and missed completely. He caught the corner and ricocheted off, to the floor. And then strutted away. And instead of finding him funny and endearing, as I usually do, I sat there loathing him. Because a cat who can't do any of the things a cat is meant to do is really just a freak, especially if he's been neutered. You see.

MARTIN: I'm sorry. I don't follow. You're surely not comparing yourself to Dennis?

STUART: Well, I certainly don't do any of the things I'm meant to do—and come on, Martin, you know why I came in with you as well as I do. To have children comfortably at your expense. And there's a lot wrong with that on any terms, but especially if, like Dennis, I can't produce any children to justify it—justify it at least partially.

MARTIN: But you will, why shouldn't you? After all, Marigold's been pregnant once.

STUART: Yes, well that was obviously something of a miracle. So what we aborted might well have been the second coming. We're not going to have them.

MARTIN: But how can you know?

84

STUART: I'm sterile. We had some tests done. Apparently I produce a mere million sperm, when only a hundred million or so will do. So her pregnancy was a miracle, you see. Medically speaking. And it's not going to be repeated, is it? Or it ceases to be a miracle, which is what is required. *(Laughs slightly)* The effect of this news has been to render me impotent as well, by the way. But that's likely to be only a passing phase. Once I stop worrying about being sterile, I'll probably become potent again. So they tell me. Anyway, that's one of the reasons why things haven't been too good between Marigold and myself recently, as you've no doubt noticed. I know you have as you've been more than usually terrific, even by your own high standards of delicacy and so forth.

MARTIN: I'm terribly sorry, I'm terribly sorry. But I beg you, don't make a decision now. At least not yet. I'm sure we can come to some arrangement. Have you discussed it with Marigold?

STUART: Not yet. Martin, having put almost all my cards on the table, I might as well plonk down the last one. Apropos of dinner tonight, really. I should quit for your sake, too, you know. You shouldn't go on just being part of a trio living for other people. You really need to be your own person at last—you do, Martin. It's time you were free of us.

(There is a silence between them. MARIGOLD *enters. She is carrying a briefcase as well as a shoulder bag)*

MARIGOLD: Hello, you both. You're looking very somber—anything the matter?

STUART: Not at all. We were—just speculating about your career prospects as a matter of fact.

MARIGOLD: And did you reach any conclusions?

STUART: That depends rather on whether you've become an assistant headmistress.

MARIGOLD: Ah, then you can go back to speculating. I won't know for a couple of days at the earliest.

MARTIN: I expect you need a drink.

STUART: I'll get it. I'm better at the preferred proportions. You tend to over do the gin and under do the lime, Marigold recently confided to me. Oh, Christ, we're out of lime.

MARTIN: I got some more; it's in the carrier bag there. But how did it go, the interview?

MARIGOLD: Oh, it was all right, I suppose. Headmistress was her usual grumpy self, but she was quite sweet really —she always is when it comes down to it. And all the others seemed friendly enough.

STUART: What sort of questions did they ask?

MARIGOLD: Oh, very conventional. You know, whether I approved of team games, and keeping Latin compulsory, what I thought of contraceptive advice for the over-six-teens, would I be prepared to take on the school play and other such stuff. I don't really want this. *(Putting down drink)* It's still too early to eat, I suppose. Where are we going to dinner, the Greek place?

STUART: Are you all right?

MARIGOLD: Yes, yes, fine—fine—just a mite peckish from nerves, probably, that's all.

STUART: Then let's go somewhere—somewhere special, what do you say to L'Epicure?

MARIGOLD: Lovely. *(To* MARTIN*)* Your favorite.

MARTIN: Yes, but actually I won't be joining you, I'm afraid.

MARIGOLD: Oh. Why not?

MARTIN: Well, because I—I—Peter entangled me in one of his alibis and before I knew what was happening I found myself having to have dinner with him and someone called Jane Papworth. Or is it him and Erika I'm having dinner with? Anyway I'd better get a move on, if I'm going to make it out to—to Hampstead in time—so I'll leave you to close shop. Good night. *(Goes to door)*

MARIGOLD *(Unable to stop herself):* Don't go!

(MARTIN *and* STUART *look at her, look at each other)*

STUART: Darling, what is it? Has something happened?

MARIGOLD *(Takes a drink):* Sorry. I seem to need this after all. I'm sorry. Sorry. I didn't go to the interview; I've been walking all afternoon. You see—you see—Martin and I. We've been having an affair.

STUART *(After a pause):* Yes, I've had a feeling—a kind of —of thought at the back of my—my mind. How long has it been going on?

MARTIN *(To* MARIGOLD): Why are you doing this?

MARIGOLD: Because I've just discovered that I am pregnant.

STUART: Of course. And you wanted to tell the husband and the father in the same breath, so to speak. *(To* MARTIN) Well, congratulations.

(NICK *enters. He is smoking an enormous cigar. He coughs)*

NICK: This is a mistake. My agent gets them free on Concorde; she dishes them out as school prizes when we've done well. So you'll gather that the answer is yes, I am about to be a television star. You shall have the first kiss from a celebrity soon *(He kisses* MARIGOLD), being my all-time favorite lady and first real love, I your chevalier. Before I break the bad news. Nappies has got the job too. We're going to be co-bloody presenting. Can you believe it! Apparently the BBC, the Boring Buggers Corporation, thinks Nappies and I complement each other, my brio striking off his lumpishness, I assume, so it'll be over to Nappies for analysis, back to me for liveliness sort of stuff, but once they go over to me they won't be going over to him very often, I'll see to that. In fact I intend to make this my chance to wipe Nappies out of public life and back to wanking poesy, where he belongs, and I'll tell you something else, his agent told my agent—*(He stops)* —is something the matter? A death been announced, or something? *(Looking around)*

MARTIN: Nick, do you think you could go?

NICK: You want me to go?

STUART: Yes, Nick, please.

NICK *(After a pause):* Oh. Right. *(He exits)*

(The sound of NICK *going down the stairs. A door slams. There is a pause. The phone rings)*

STUART *(Lets it ring, then answers it):* Yes. Oh hello, Erika. Yes, it is. No, Peter's gone, I'm afraid. *(Little pause)* Yes, he is. *(Listens, and then to* MARTIN*)* Erika's baby-sitter's let her down. So she won't be able to join you and Peter for dinner tonight. She's sorry if she's caused any problems. *(Into phone)* Right, he's got that. *(Little pause)* Very well, thank you—yes, Marigold too, but Erika, I really can't talk now, we're in a—a rather important meeting with an author. See you soon. Bye. *(Hangs up)*

(There is a pause. STUART *looks at* MARIGOLD, *then at* MARTIN*)*

MARTIN: I'm sorry.

STUART: No, you're not.

MARTIN *(After a pause):* No, I'm not. How could I be? I've never wanted anyone else in my life. From the first moment I saw her. I've never loved anyone else. Apart from you. So I'm sorry I've brought you—brought you hurt is what I meant. Of all people. If it had been yours, I'd have loved it, but as it's mine—

STUART: Shut up! Shut up! *(Moving toward him. Checks himself)* I haven't got your capacity for decency, loyalty, etc.; as it's yours, I want to kill it. And you. *(To* MARIGOLD*)* And you. As a matter of fact. *(Stands staring at her)* I've no intention of letting you go. I love you too much. And we've spent far too many years—many years —*(Turns suddenly away, goes and sits down)*

MARIGOLD *(Stares at him):* Oh, my love! *(Little pause)* Oh, my love! *(Runs to him, puts her arms around him)*

LIGHTS OUT

SCENE 2

MARTIN*'s office. A few years later. Late autumn. About 6:30 in the evening. Thin sunshine through the windows. The office door is open.* MARTIN*'s jacket is over the back of his desk* *chair.* STUART's *old desk is still there, but at a different angle, no longer directly facing* MARTIN's.

There is a bottle of whisky on MARTIN's *desk, and a glass with some whisky in it.*

NICK *is in the armchair, a drink in his hand.* PETER *is sitting at* MARTIN's *desk, feet on desk, a drink in his hand.*

PETER: What a bugger funerals are! Eh? Especially for atheists.

NICK *(After a pause):* Why doesn't somebody do "Fear no more—"?

PETER: Fear no more what?

NICK: "Fear no more the heat of the sun / Nor the furious winter's rages, / Thou thy worldy task hast done / Home art gone and ta'en they wages. / Golden lads and girls all must / As chimney sweepers, come to— *(He wheezes uncontrollably, starts to cough violently. Sits breathing heavily, clearly shaken)*

PETER: I thought you'd been ordered to stop.

NICK: Well, I still hold to my life's single principle. You don't live longer, it just seems— *(He coughs again rackingly)*

(The sound of footsteps, coming up the stairs)

91

PETER: But you'll never know, will you, how long it might have been. If you go on like this.

NICK: No. That's an extra perk.

MARTIN *(Enters, in his shirt-sleeves):* I was absolutely sure I heard footsteps. And there was an odd smell at the bottom of the stairs. Of alcohol and hospitals. Probably some old wino staggered in for a moment, I suppose.

PETER: Or the ghost of Hubert Stout come on ahead.

MARTIN: One ghost is enough for the evening. Anyway, I've left the door unlocked—so if he *does* turn up . . . he'll be able to get in. He probably didn't even get the message on his answering machine. He might still be in the States for all I know. What train *(To* PETER) are you catching?

PETER: I promised Jane I'd get the seven-forty. The ghastly Erika's dumping the kids on us for the weekend. It's sheer malice, as she's got nothing better to do than look after them, which is all she's ever been up to anyway. And Jane can't dump her lot on bloody Papworth as he's away at some theological conference giving his now famous lecture about me—Judas as Adulterer. I sometimes think I should get a cut of his fees. So there are going to be seven kids—eight, with the baby, who seems to have discovered a method of going without sleep entirely, by the way, and what with all the catering, the bed-making, the quarrels over sleeping bags, et cetera, Jane made me promise I'd get back on the seven-forty.

Act Two

NICK: I was just saying, what about "Fear no more"?

MARTIN: What?

PETER: The dirge. From *Cymbeline*. Nick's idea is to recite the first few lines and cough himself to death. And then we could have a double funeral. He's got emphysema.

MARTIN: Emphysema. You're an idiot, Nick.

PETER: How do you manage to control it on your dreadful television program? Or do they cut to Nappies whenever you cough? I've noticed his appearances have been getting longer and longer.

NICK: Actually, Nappies is leaving the Boring Buggers Corporation. He's going to be theater critic on the *Sunday Times*. Apparently they're impressed by his lack of qualifications. But he's under the impression I'll allow him back now and then as my guest, to read out some of his wankings. We're having dinner to celebrate. Five minutes ago.

MARTIN: I'm going to be publishing Nappies, did I tell you? His collected poems.

NICK: Really, well he's not a bad poet, a bit derivative, but that's what he should stick to. As a matter of fact, I'll miss him. One needs someone one hates meshed into the texture of one's life.

MARTIN: Well, has anyone come up with any more ideas?

93

NICK: Well, we can do anything we like really these days, can't we? The last funeral I went to was my aunt's. They played a selection of ballroom waltzes. She'd asked for them especially.

PETER: I imagine she'd have to. After all, it isn't something a vicar would have the wit to think up by himself. Look, we're not really getting anywhere, and I haven't much time. Why don't we just stick to playing some Wagner and read some . . .

(Sound of footsteps. They look toward the door. STUART *enters)*

STUART: Sorry. I only got in an hour ago—the flight was late as usual. And there was only half your message. Something seems to have gone wrong with my answering machine again.

(There is a pause)

MARTIN: You got the bit about Humpty though, did you?

STUART: Only that he was dead. What happened? Was it suicide?

PETER: Sort of.

MARTIN: He was murdered. A young man he picked up in the Cambridge marketplace. Humpty took him back and—*(He gestures)*

94

NICK: Apparently Humpty didn't put up much of a fight. Just let himself be beaten to death.

MARTIN: He was naked, apparently.

PETER: Except for a sock.

MARTIN: We'd heard what he was getting up to. The risks he was taking. We all tried to warn him, but it was almost as if he *wanted* to be murdered. Oh, but you must need a drink.

STUART: Yes. Thanks. *(He gets a glass)*

PETER: Yes, well, he certainly seems to have anticipated it. For one thing he left some stuff. In an envelope. A letter to me. And some poems.

MARTIN: Yes, there are about a dozen. Apparently he'd just started writing again. Anyway, we're meeting because of his father. The mother died last year and he's, what, nearly eighty. He asked me if I'd organize the funeral. He wants to do the right thing, you see. And he wants to have something characteristic of Humphry, whom he obviously didn't know very well. He kept saying, "The sock, I don't understand about the sock." We've got to decide tonight as the college wants to know what we've planned. The master and some of the fellows intend to come to the service.

PETER: I should think so too. For a senior moral tutor.

MARTIN: So far we've had proposals of a brief reading of those poems he wouldn't let you publish when he was an undergraduate—and the new poems, if you think they're any good, of course. And an extract from the introduction to the Wagner book he never wrote. And—um—

NICK: The dirge from *Cymbeline.*

STUART: Surely Humphry would have wanted whatever his father would have wanted.

PETER: Well, what would that be?

STUART: I should think the traditional Church of England service in the traditional version.

(A pause)

MARTIN: Yes, of course. I'm sure that's right.

PETER: Yes.

MARTIN: I suppose one of us should make a short memorial speech, though. *(To* STUART*)* Will you do it, Stuart?

STUART: Well, actually I think Peter should, as he's the one of us Humpty really cared about.

PETER: Yes, I had an idea it would end up with me. All right.

NICK *(Getting up):* So that's settled then? Oh, by the way, Stuart, terrific that your Hubert Stout biography is doing so well—did you get a message from your agent about appearing on our show—my show from now on?

STUART: Yes, I did. Thanks, Nick. Can I think it over?

NICK: Yes of course, but don't worry, I'll do you proud. I'll give you the main slot. All I ask is that you keep it anecdotal. Your own experience of Stout, things you found out from his friends, his various marriages, mistresses, and other messes, his school days—that sort of thing. Most of our audience won't know anything about his poems, but we can make them interested in his life, if we go about it the right way. And the thing is, it'll be a big plug for your book, won't it?

STUART: I know, and I'll certainly think about it, Nick. Thanks.

NICK: Look, let's have lunch and talk about it properly. I've got to be off. I mustn't keep Nappies waiting more than the usual half an hour. He might take offense and stay on the program.

PETER: Where are you having dinner?

NICK: Notting Hill Gate.

PETER: Good. Can I come with you? You can drop me at the station.

NICK: Right. Bye, Martin.

MARTIN: Bye.

97

PETER: It's a good book, Stuart. Bloody well researched too. You really got the goods on him, although in the end I was actually quite moved. Anyway, I wish I could write something like that. Although I still don't understand the poems.

STUART: Congratulations on the job at Leeds, by the way. I meant to drop you a note.

PETER: It's a dump. But at least I'll be a professor—the fifth youngest in the country, as a matter of fact, and I'll be earning twice the money which I need. Oh, Erika sends her love, by the way.

STUART: Erika?

PETER: I mean Jane, of course. Sorry. *(Little embarrassed laugh)* So next time you're in Oxford—Leeds, that is, from next term—

STUART: Right.

NICK *(From the door):* Come on, Peter, if you're coming.

(PETER, NICK *exit. Sound of* NICK *coughing. There is a pause)*

MARTIN: So how was New York?

STUART: O.K. A lot of lectures, interviews, all that. Like Nick, they're not much interested in Stout's poetry. Only his life. The marriages, mistresses, and messes in other words.

MARTIN: I had the impression that you didn't like him very much by the time you'd finished.

STUART: I found out rather more than I wanted to know, you see.

MARTIN: Oh. Here's Humpty's stuff. I'm thinking of publishing the poems. Perhaps you'd do the introduction.

STUART: Right.

MARTIN: Look, I've got to go. *(Slight hesitation)* We're having dinner out for once. L'Epicure. Our baby-sitter, Michelle, by the way, our first secretary, remember? —doesn't allow us out late. She's retaking her university entrance; she very nearly got a place last time . . . so if you want to stay and finish your drink—and lock up after. You don't need a key—but you know the procedure.

STUART *(Smiles):* How is Marigold?

MARTIN: She's fine. She likes being headmistress, although it's a bit tiring. A bit of trouble with her father. That's normal of course. *(Little pause)* He was caught shoplifting.

STUART: Oh. And the twins?

MARTIN: They're fine.

STUART: Good. And Samantha and Dennis?

MARTIN: Yes. I'm afraid we've had to have them put down. The twins are asthmatic, you see, and they were too old to find a new home for.

(STUART *nods*)

MARTIN: We're moving out of here. We're looking for premises on two floors.

STUART: I'm sure that's the right thing to do.

MARTIN: Might you come and see Marigold and the twins one day? She'd like that.

STUART: Oh, one day I'm sure I will.

(MARTIN *picks up his glass, holds it out to* STUART)

MARTIN: Humpty, eh?

STUART: Yes, Humpty. *(He lifts his glass. Both drink)*

MARTIN *(Little pause):* Do you think he was the best of us? I've been wondering that since it happened.

STUART: Well, he didn't mess up any lives except his own, I suppose. Except—I suppose the poor sod he probably provoked into murdering him. Have they caught him, by the way?

MARTIN: Oh, yes. Trying to sell Humpty's hi-fi and a whole stack of his records. He didn't give himself a chance. *(He drains off his glass)* Well then, if not the best, then the first to go. If Nick doesn't look out, he'll be next.

STUART: So, it happened in his rooms, did it?

MARTIN: Mmmm?

STUART: Humphry's murder.

MARTIN: Yes, in his rooms.

STUART: My old rooms, in fact.

MARTIN: So they were. *(Little pause)* Please come and see us. She misses you dreadfully, of course. *(He turns, and goes out quickly)*

STUART *goes to* MARTIN'*s desk, looks at it, then crosses to his old desk. He turns on the desk light, takes the poems out of the envelope, puts on his glasses, glances at the poems, still standing. Strains of Wagner, in full and majestic flow, towards the end side of the record from Act I, Scene 1)*

LIGHTS OUT

EPILOGUE

STUART's *room in Cambridge. Twenty years ago exactly where it left off in Act I, Scene 1. Wagner is in full and majestic flow.* MARTIN *is still in his intensely listening posture.* PETER *is sitting, casually, looking through a pocket diary.* HUMPHRY *is watching* NICK, *who is lying on the bed, conducting and humming along with Wagner.* MARIGOLD *enters*

MARIGOLD: Hello, everybody.

PETER: Shazam! Where have you been?

MARIGOLD: Sorry we're late. Stuart is just coming. He's just saying good-bye to Hubert Stout.

NICK: Hubert Stout! Do you mean to say that while we've been seething passionately away in here, close to fisticuffs from time to time, you two have been calmly having it off with Hubert Stout! And you didn't even bring him over and introduce him!

MARIGOLD: Yes, I know, I'm sorry. But you see we saw him crossing the court to one of the guest rooms. So we decided to nobble him. So we knocked on his door and when he opened it, we just barged in and Stuart began telling him about the magazine as if he'd known him all his life. The thing is, he was very, very interested. Wanted to know all about contributors, how we were going to organize subscriptions, but most of all how many pages we were going to give to poetry.

(STUART *enters the room*)

MARIGOLD: And he said he might even give us a poem.

STUART: Well actually, he didn't go quite that far. But the point is, the real point is, that meeting him today seemed like a sort of omen. A portent. I told him it was going to be called *The Common Pursuit;* he liked that. He's a great admirer of Leavis, though of course he has his reservations. But he said that it would establish what our critical standards were. That we were serious, in other words. So he's already on our side, you see. Oh, Marigold, have you been introduced to Humphry Taylor, who sent in the poems I told you about? Marigold Watson.

MARIGOLD: Hello.

STUART: And of course you've already met, um, um . . . I'm terribly sorry.

MARTIN: Martin Musgrove.

STUART: Who's offered to take over the advertising, business, et cetera.

MARTIN *(To* MARIGOLD, *smiles):* All the really boring stuff, in fact, is my level.

STUART: Right. Let's get started.

HUMPHRY: As a matter of fact, I've just come to pick up my poems.

STUART: What? But why?

HUMPHRY: Because I don't like them anymore.

STUART: But they're very good. In fact, they're remarkable. Every time I read them, I find something new in them. You must let the magazine have them.

HUMPHRY: I'm sorry. I don't want to see them published.

STUART: Look, can I talk to you about them properly? Just the two of us. You mustn't make a decision now. Please . . .

NICK: There is going to be a theater column, isn't there?

STUART: I'm not sure, but I have an idea it wouldn't be appropriate.

NICK: Well, if we don't have a theater page, can we have a sex page? Marigold and I can edit together, can't we, Marigold? And we'll publish pictures of Captain Marvel having it off with ghastly Erika. If I choose to introduce them.

HUMPHRY: I thought this was going to be serious.

NICK (*To* MARTIN): Shhhh!

Act Two

STUART: What we need to talk about now isn't simply what we want for our first few issues but our whole future. One very important thing Hubert Stout said is that, above all, we've got to be very careful. Take into account all the things that could go wrong, all the traps that other people have fallen into when starting out on something like this. That's the only way we'll survive. By knowing what it is we are about to give the world, precisely.

MARIGOLD: Absolutely.

MARTIN: Yes. Absolutely.

(Lights)

CURTAIN